HIGHER THAN I

Thanks Paddy.

I hope this book encourages your desire to find purpose in your times of reflection.

Blessings,

Rob.

HIGHER THAN I

*Meditations for
Spiritual Direction*

ROB DES COTES

CLEMENTS PUBLISHING
Toronto

Published 2007 by Clements Publishing
6021 Yonge Street, Box 213
Toronto, Ontario M2M 3W2 Canada
www.clementspublishing.com

Unless otherwise noted, all Scripture quotations are from the
HOLY BIBLE, NEW INTERNATIONAL VERSION
copyright © 1973, 1978, 1984 by the International Bible Society.

Cover design by Rob Clements and Rob Des Cotes

Library and Archives Canada Cataloguing in Publication

Des Cotes, Rob, 1954-
Higher than I : meditations for spiritual direction / Rob Des Cotes.

Includes bibliographical references and index.
ISBN-10: 1-894667-67-0
ISBN-13: 978-1-894667-67-8

1. Bible—Meditations. 2. Spiritual direction—Christianity—
Meditations.

I. Title.

BS491.5.D483 2007   242'.5
C2007-903128-5

CONTENTS

INTRODUCTION

A S with our first offering, *Fan the Flame*, these meditations were not primarily written for the purpose of publishing a book. They originated as weekly encouragements, prompts for discussion, written for our various Imago Dei communities which presently exist in locations throughout British Columbia, Canada (www.imagodeicommunity.ca), as well as for the many people around the world—the Friends of Imago Dei—who are on our e-mail list. These writings are the result of a natural process that has much in common with indigenous art-making in that they have been created both *for* community, as well as *from* community.

The meditations in this book reflect something of the week-to-week concerns of a fellowship intent on continual growth and transformation in the Spirit of Christ. The issues they deal with are not theoretical, but ones which we face in our own lives as we wrestle with the counter-spiritual influences within and around us. In these struggles however we also live in anticipation of grace as we give ourselves, more and more, to God's action in our lives.

Although each of these meditations is prefaced by a biblical Scripture they are not necessarily exegetical studies of those particular passages. Rather, the biblical text serves as an anchor as well as a point of departure for considering the particular application of spiritual principles in our lives that these passages, either directly or obliquely, imply. How does one truly seek God? What does it mean to literally follow the Lord's leading in our lives? What are the obstacles we face in this? How can we grow to become more and more available to God's creative purposes in and through us? These are some of the questions of spiritual direction that we are in dialogue with Scripture over.

Our work with Imago Dei is built on the premise that God invites each one of us to be transformed daily into that which more perfectly reflects His will, and that it is the responsibility of each believer to bear the fruit that is possible for their own lives. Imago Dei, then, is nothing more than a "community of influence" and it is in this capacity that the book, *Higher Than I*, is offered—as an encouragement to any and all who share these simple values of spiritual direction with us. The book offers creative metaphors and insights to inspire the heart in its pursuit of God as it gleans from many sources, both ancient and contemporary, of spiritual theology.

If you find in these pages any affirmation of what the Holy Spirit has already been teaching you, any motivation for pursuing more intently your heart's desire to "seek His face," or any fellowship with others who share your most profound spiritual yearnings, the book will have served every purpose we would pray for it. May the Lord bless us with hungering hearts.

Rob Des Cotes
Thanksgiving, Oct. 8, 2007
Vancouver, B.C.

MEDITATIONS FOR SPIRITUAL DIRECTION

1

Lead me to the rock that is higher than I.

Psalm 61:2

The Presence of God is the very origin and wellspring of life itself. It is no wonder then, that to draw near this Presence is to approach the most fertile place in existence, and to draw away from it is to move in the direction of non-growth, which ultimately leads to death.

A lot of what Jesus had to say about the kingdom of heaven had to do with how things prosper and bear good fruit because of their proximity to God. To be close to Jesus, the true vine, is synonymous with growth, and conversely, spiritual growth in our lives is a sign that we are living in the realm of God's kingdom.

It is possible however to stop growing in our faith. We find ourselves on a plateau of spirituality, assuming that the depth of relationship we have experienced with God thus far is all that the Christian life has to offer. But thankfully, the Lord has made this conclusion an uncomfortable one for us. More often than not we feel restless in our spirits as we pine for an experience of spiritual life that is greater than the one we presently have. And the very fact that we hunger for more is evidence of the Spirit's activity within us.

Before a next stage of growth occurs, God often instills a deep desire for change in us. This sets up a momentum for growth that continues to thrive long after the initial spurt. Many saints have identified how desire for God leads not only to satisfaction, but often to an even greater experience of desire. Hungering and thirsting then are signs of a deepening relationship with God. They represent the outreach of the soul for its next stage of maturity. To simply have this desire for growth is to participate with divinity.

Julian of Norwich, a 14th-century mystic, once received a word from the Lord that helped identify this relationship to the God-granted desire within her. In one of her many "showings," the Lord revealed Himself to Julian saying, "I am the ground of thy beseeching. If I caused you to beseech, will I not also grant you the object of your beseeching?"

The desire by which Julian was led to seek God was also the evidence that the object of her desire was within reach. God caused her to long for union with Him, and this longing itself was the God-given assurance that her desire would inevitably be fulfilled.

Consider the spiritual desires that you presently experience, and reflect on how God has placed these within you in order to cause you to seek Him. Our deep longings, far from revealing inadequacy, can be welcomed as precious gifts, tokens of what is to come in their satisfaction.

2

As the deer pants for streams of water,
so my soul pants for you, O God.
My soul thirsts for God, for the living God.

Psalm 42:1-2

We are, by nature, desiring beings. We can't help it. And though our attachments to our desires often work against us, they can also serve God's purposes in leading us towards union with Him. We are used to thinking of attachment, especially in its extreme forms of addiction, in negative terms but there is also a positive form of addiction where similar features of craving as well as the discomfort of withdrawal can actually work in us for the good of the soul.

As easy as it is to become addicted to external stimulants we can also be addicted to our inner moods and dispositions—depression, shyness, fear, anger, cynicism. As we habitually favour these responses to life, our psychology and our physiology naturally default to them in a given situation. This is the negative side of our inner attachments. But this same principle of habituation to a particular inner state can also apply to our being "attached" to positive behaviours.

People who regularly practice prayer, for instance, find that their mind, body and soul become more and more identified with this inner state of spirit. It becomes a "mood" that they come to expect as a norm in their lives. Once the state of prayer becomes established as a norm we also begin to recognize symptoms of withdrawal—a longing, or craving to return to what is familiar—if we depart from that norm for too long. Our physiology will register discomfort whenever our prayerful inner state has been neglected for a longer than usual period. Of course, if we continue to remain absent from a regular prayer pattern it will eventually establish a new norm for us—one that presumes that prayer is the foreign state rather than the normal one.

The more we understand the principle of habituation the more we can apply it positively to our lives. We can intentionally choose to habituate ourselves to whatever we consider beneficial. It takes a little time and intentionality but, once our physiology gets over the initial resistance to a new behaviour, it will eventually habituate to it as a new norm. Once so, it will not only anticipate the new disposition each day, but will even crave it when it is absent. Our physiology will then serve to help us stay on track by alerting us, through the uncomfortable symptoms of withdrawal, whenever we neglect the new habit that we've established.

In a nutshell, we are attached to whatever makes things normal for us. The longer a norm continues, the more things will become associated with it and the more entrenched it will be in our lives. This is a useful principle that we can apply positively to whatever we deem beneficial as we seek to become more and more habituated to the norms of a spiritual life.

3

You need to persevere so that when you have done the will of God, you will receive what he has promised.

Heb. 10:36

Perhaps the spiritual life *is* like rocket science after all. Its goals are just as far-reaching and, with every failed attempt, the reasons for quitting seem just as compelling. If you've ever seen the movie *October Sky* you'll remember the homemade rockets that, for a few seconds, carried the hopes of being propelled all the way to outer space only to peter out and fizzle a few hundred meters off the ground. Sound familiar? What is it that motivated rocket scientists to persevere in spite of so many setbacks if it wasn't the certain faith that, one way or another, outer space was within reach. How many times must we too go back to the drawing board before we see the results we hope for in our spiritual life?

A new insight often grips us with fresh motivation and a commitment to aspire to what it indicates possible. We suddenly find it easy to envision change and, with that fresh wind, we feel the incentive to try new ways or to adopt new practices. Perhaps we've read Brother Lawrence's *The Practice of the Presence of God.* We've tasted something of how simple the spiritual life can be, and it's inspired us to cultivate such attentiveness in our day. Or perhaps, in a sudden epiphany, we've come to recognize once again how every person is uniquely loved by God, and we immediately want to start including that insight in all our encounters. Maybe we've come to a deeper appreciation of prayer, of its essential relationship to progress in the spiritual life, and we feel a renewed dedication to making more for time for it in our week.

In these and many other initiatives we usually begin strong as we zealously set out in the direction of transformation. Visionary courage becomes the fuel that puts our faith into motion. And, with our rocket launched, we watch with hope as it reaches out towards its goals. But what happens once the immediate enthusiasm has gone, when our rocket peters out and lands unceremoniously back on the ground?

Discouragement (lit. *loss of heart*) is the fizzling of visionary courage that first accompanied our resolve. Rather than staying the course and keeping to our inspired path, we feel frustrated by our apparent failure and are tempted to give up. How we respond to this experience determines much of our future course. Perhaps we feel more hesitant to ever make such resolutions again lest we risk failure. Or perhaps we begin to rationalize our setback in a way that makes genuine enthusiasm less possible. "I guess I'm not cut out for this." "Surely this practice is not necessary for everyone." "Maybe I was being too idealistic." "Others have more time for this stuff than God can expect from me."

But what if the experience of frustration, far from being grounds for quitting, were actually an essential part of the journey. What greater distance could we travel if our first resolve was to never let go of our initial hopes? Discouragement would then be just a temporary, but necessary state that we only have to bear with until the next updraft.

Experience teaches us that if we hold on to our first hope, courage will likely return and once again fuel our faith into action. Like rocket science, perseverance will pay off and, sooner or later, our spiritual hopes will break free from the forces of gravity that keep them earthbound.

We must not break the strings nor throw out the lute when we find
a discord; we must bend our ear to find where the disorder comes
from, and then gently tighten or relax the string as required.

St. Frances de Sales

4

For Satan himself masquerades as an angel of light.

2 Cor.11:14

Do hardships, closed doors, persecution, or inner turmoil mean that you are moving away from the Lord's direction in your life? Maybe, maybe not. Does the experience of inner peace, of all things coming together, of unimpeded progress necessarily mean that the Lord is blessing your life's direction? Maybe, maybe not.

How we experience our life's circumstances, in itself, is not enough to determine whether we are on the right path or not. So taught St. Ignatius of Loyola who wisely recognized that our relative experiences of peace or disquiet in life might have as much to do with which direction we are facing than with the leading of the Lord. Our enemy can just as easily lead us through experiences of both peace or disquiet

St. Ignatius, in his *Spiritual Exercises*, puts it this way,

Both the good angel and the evil spirit can give consolation to a soul, but for quite different purposes. The good angel consoles for the progress of the soul, that it may advance and rise to what is more perfect. The evil spirit consoles for purposes that are the contrary.

All consolations are not necessarily from God and it is important that we not run too far ahead on that assumption. The *Spiritual Exercises* counsels that if we are in a state of consolation we should continue to discern the effect this state of soul is having on us throughout the evolution of its fruit. It is quite possible that something which starts off as a consolation can later leads us astray. At times, according to Ignatius, the "evil angel" can even appear to be walking in agreement with our virtues only to be better able to pervert them later.

It is a mark of the evil spirit to assume the appearance of an angel of light. He begins by suggesting thoughts that are suited to a devout soul, and ends by suggesting his own.

On its own, an experience of peace does not give us enough information to determine whether it is the Lord who is leading us or not. We need to also ask which direction we are facing at the time of the experience. This, more than anything else, will determine how we experience either the influence of God or the influence of an evil spirit. Are we in a season of drawing nearer to God, or are we moving away from God? Our experiences of the good spirit or the evil spirit will differ accordingly. According to St. Ignatius, whenever there is vitality in our spiritual direction we will likely experience the actions of both spirits as follows,

In souls that are progressing to greater perfection, the action of the good angel is delicate, gentle, delightful. It may be compared to a drop of water penetrating a sponge. The action of the evil spirit upon such souls is violent, noisy and disturbing. It may be compared to a drop of water falling on a stone.

However, if we are moving away from God, Ignatius observes how we will experience the very opposite.

In souls that are going from bad to worse, the action of the spirits as mentioned above is just the reverse. The reason for this is due to either the opposition or similarity of these souls to the differ- ent kinds of spirits. When the disposition of the soul is contrary to that of the spirit, they appear to enter in with noise and commotion that are easily perceived. When the disposition is similar to that of the spirits, they enter silently, as one coming into his own house when the doors are open,

Depending on which spiritual direction we are facing we will appear more or less hospitable to the Spirit of God—either welcoming His gentle promptings and corrections, or else feeling irritated or at odds with His counsel. The same is true of the evil spirit. One way or another, we are inevitably spiritual hosts. And being honest about which direction we are facing can at least give us opportunity to wisely discern which spirits we are to welcome, and which ones we should be inhospitable to.

5

You have laid down precepts that are to be fully obeyed.

Psalm 119:4

In *Theologia Germanica*, a 14th-century manuscript that Martin Luther considered second only to the Bible, the anonymous author speaks of four different relationships one can have to the law. It's easy to recognize aspects of ourselves in each of these four dispositions, and perhaps this medieval wisdom can help us understand what it means to be in right relationship to God's precepts.

The author presents the first relationship as that of a person who sees the law as a regrettable, but necessary constraint in life. People who have this type of relationship with laws, be they civil, spiritual or self-prescribed, try to have as little as possible to do with them, seeing them as a hindrance that they would rather avoid in life. They acknowledge the law, but wish it weren't there.

The second relationship to laws and precepts is the one that assumes reward, as in the case of the person who thinks of gaining credit or approval by keeping them. People who follow this second way are unfortunately also the ones who most live in fear of breaking a law. Rules and disciplines become for them an external taskmaster and they fear the consequences of stepping out of line with what has been prescribed. The burden of obedience is heavy for these people and they need to be encouraged towards a different disposition. As the author of the *Theologia Germanica* writes, "to serve God and to live for Him is easy to whoever does it for love, but it is hard and wearisome to anyone who does it for hire" (TG 38) We must always remember that Jesus invites to be His friends, not His slaves.

A third way of relating to the law is to simply ignore it—to side step it completely as though it were not needed, or did not apply to our lives— an approach that neither the author, nor the Scriptures recommend. This form of anarchy mocks those, including God, who value laws and ordinances, by attempting to "enter the gate" by some other means than the demands of obedience that Jesus Himself modeled for us.

The fourth and preferred way is that practiced by those who follow the law, not for reward, nor from any constraint or guilt, but because they recognize that the law is good. They obey God's precepts for the simple reason that they love the ways of the Lord. Like the psalmist, their disposition in life is one that proclaims, "Oh, how I love your law! I meditate on it all day long." (Ps. 119:97)

In this disposition, Jesus recognizes us acting as friends of the law, not as hirelings. In agreement with God—that His law is good—we finally experience the relational freedom that friends are meant to enjoy.

> *You are my friends if you do what I command. I no longer call you servants, because a servant does not know his master's business. Instead, I have called you friends, for everything that I learned from my Father I have made known to you.*
>
> John 15:14-15

6

> *Now He was telling them a parable to show that at all times they ought to pray and not to lose heart. (or, "not to faint," KJV)*
>
> Luke 18:1(NASB)

Like most of us, when it comes to keeping a tab on my soul I seem to be prone to chronic spiritual amnesia. Jesus, in this passage, prescribes an antidote for this type of forgetfulness—"at all times they ought to pray." Prayer, the Lord teaches us, helps keep our spiritual heart at the forefront of our lives. It keeps us from falling asleep or fainting by helping us stay awake to the *fact* of our souls.

Often, when I am in prayer, I feel that I am recovering something essential to my being. Prayer helps me return to a place of truth that I had wandered away from without even knowing it. Only after I have once again found myself in this way do I realize how absent I have been from my true self. Maybe it's from overly identifying with my thought life, or perhaps it's the busy pace of a day that is at fault, but it seems that awareness of my spirit-life often follows the old adage of "out of sight, out of mind." The focus of prayer helps me identify once again what and where my soul is. As I rediscover my "heart of hearts" I am reminded of its place as the centre of who I really am. It seems that God has to keep recovering this basic truth for me—that I come from a much deeper place within myself than I think I do. I also sense that, ultimately, the Lord wants me to be operating from this deeper place at all times.

Prayer cultivates sensitivity to the spiritual life that is always active at the core of our being. It's no wonder that Jesus tells us that we ought to always pray—so that we won't lose sight of what is essential to our lives. This is the prescription that the Great Physician recommends for the recovery of our souls. We would be wise to follow it and even wiser, once we have recovered our heart, to learn how to not lose it again.

7

I am the LORD your God; consecrate yourselves and be holy, because I am holy.

Lev. 11:44

Can you picture yourself as a saint? Jesus certainly can and, by the grace of the Holy Spirit, He is focusing this image more and more in you, as the goal of your life. Grace abounds in order to convince us that this identity is not only possible in us, but inevitable.

In a class I teach on Contemplative Traditions we spoke of the fruit that a life-long discipline in contemplative prayer would bear in a person, and how such fruit might benefit the world. The class, mostly fourth-year university students, were asked to picture themselves in the twilight years of their lives. Could they imagine themselves as wise old men and women who knew, first-hand, the truth of a life-long intimacy with God? Can you picture that for yourself? Can you see how your spiritual work today contributes to that future person you will one day be?

Holiness, as a pursuit and a destination for our lives, is of prime importance to God because it implies fellowship with what is most intrinsic to His own character. He would have us be as He is. It is, after all, what we were made to be. To consider this call seriously is to engage with the very heartbeat of spiritual direction within us.

Be holy as I am holy. The fact that holiness is of paramount importance to God is reason enough for it to be so for us. Being holy isn't a work that we can achieve or even envision on our own. But to grow in our desire for holiness certainly is—to prize it as God prizes it.

Jesus once taught that "where your treasure is your heart will follow (Matt. 6:21)." If we carry the hope of holiness within us, if we sincerely desire purity of heart, and if we long to see sanctification in our life, we can be sure that our heart, soul, and life will follow where our treasure lies.

> *Make every effort... to be holy; without holiness no one will see the Lord.*
>
> Heb. 12:14

8

Train a child in the way he should go.

Prov. 22:6

One way or another, life grows. We have very little say in the *fact* that it grows, but we do have say in *how* it grows. In other words we have opportunity, as Scripture encourages, to train our life—like one would train a child—in the way it should go.

Once, in a class on spiritual formation, the instructor brought in a miniature bonsai tree to help us understand how spiritual growth is encouraged. For aesthetic as well as other reasons, limbs on a bonsai tree are trained to grow in certain ways, and discouraged from growing in others. The analogy to spiritual life is obvious.

The way a particular growth pattern in a bonsai tree is encouraged is by wiring the branches in such a way that they are pulled, as they grow, in the desired direction. It's a slow but sure process that trains the tree by channeling its growth in a preferred direction.

In order to protect the branches and to ensure that the desired outcome is achieved there are important rules to follow when wiring bonsai trees. Here are five important lessons I've learned about wiring a bonsai tree that also aptly apply to spiritual direction:

• The wire needs to remain in place for at least three months in order for the branch to become trained in the new direction. During this time the wire should never become loose.

• Care must be taken to ensure that, as the tree grows, the wire does not bite into it, causing scarring. It can take many years for wire damage to grow out. The wiring should be constantly adjusted, as growth takes place, in order to avoid this.

• Wiring works by bending the wood to the point of stressing and purposely damaging some of the cells in the former bend. The tree, while repairing the damage, now grows back according to the new shape imposed on it by the wire.

• It is pointless and potentially damaging to wire an unhealthy tree. If you wire a tree that is not in full vigour it might be unable to complete the repair and you could end up harming the branch.

• You should never wire a bonsai tree that has just been repotted. It's also important to give a tree adequate time to recover from one wiring before you begin another.

Consider how these principles apply to your own life. What "wires" do you have in place that are now directing your spiritual growth? Are they helping or hindering your growth? Are they too loose to really be productive? Or are they too tight? Do you have scars in your life from wires that have been too tight in the past? Do you feel strong enough at present to take on a new spiritual discipline or would you be wise to wait until you have more spiritual vitality?

The Book of Proverbs encourages us to "train a child in the way he should go." We apply this wisdom to ourselves as we learn to adopt beneficial "habits of the heart" that help channel our growth in a preferred direction.

In the example of a miniature bonsai tree, God shows us how easy it is to take a branch that is growing in one direction, and train it to grow in another. It's simply a matter of learning how to keep beneficial patterns in place long enough that they become the new norms for your life.

9

Be still and know that I am God

Psalm 46:10

According to this word, there is a particular knowledge of God that can only come through stillness. The dictionary defines this state as one that is "free from disturbance or agitation." To be still means to stop both our inner and outer activity in order to be attentive to what God is doing apart from our own initiatives. It provides a rare opportunity for us to get to know the Lord in ways that we would never do otherwise. Only from the point of stillness can we observe the subtle grace of God's movement touching the soul, and of our own spirit's gentle sigh for God.

The invitation to be still in God's presence sounds so wonderful but it is also very difficult to do. If prayer teaches us anything it teaches us just how agitated our spirits really are. That is why so many people over the centuries have recognized the need for spiritual discipline in cultivating the sacred art of stillness.

A form of spirituality that was characteristic in the 4th and 5th centuries is called *hesychasm*. Those who practiced this discipline were mostly hermits dwelling in the deserts, seeking inner peace and spiritual insight through contemplation, self-discipline and the study of Scriptures. The word *hesychasm* means "sacred quietude" and the practice of cultivating this inner rest and silence was seen as an essential support for prayer

The exhortation to "be still *in order* to know God" reminds us that stillness is not an end in itself. As delightful as the experience of peace might be, it is only a means to a far greater end—the particular knowledge and experience of God that it uniquely leads to.

As both philosophers and artists know, our capacity for perception is determined mostly by our point of perspective. From the point of view of stillness, we get to see ourselves, God and others in ways that we would never have opportunity to do otherwise. It is only from the place of stillness that we can perceive truth as it freely reveals itself to be.

10

He came to that which was His own.

John 1:11

In 1961, astronaut Alan Shepard, the first man to ever view the earth from space, expressed his sense of awe using the only words that seemed fitting at the time. Gazing at the beautiful gem of his home planet Shepard quoted from the first chapter of the Bible, "In the beginning, God created the heavens and the earth." Never had these words held such meaning for humans as when they were read from the perspective of that spectacular view from outer space. Something of a similar perspective is also needed in order to appreciate heaven's sense of God coming to earth in the birth of Jesus.

Jesus did much more than simply come to earth. He was not merely a visitor from afar, a foreign messenger bringing a divine word to us from above. Meteors come from above, land on the earth and are embedded in its crust. But they always remain foreign objects to us. They are never truly a part of who we are.

But Jesus not only came *to* the earth, He also came *from* it—from its own matter. In Mary's womb, Jesus' body drew the chemicals and minerals necessary for Him to grow. He, the Creator of all that exists, became a product of His own creation. And, like a seed that draws nutrients from the soil in order to become a tree, Jesus still draws from the earth all that is needed for His ministry. This is the mystery of the Incarnation that continues to unfold in and through our lives today.

God comes from within. Jesus has entered deep into the DNA of creation and the earth has never been the same. Like the images we see of scientists fertilizing cells, where DNA from one cell is injected into another, a Divine gene has been injected into the "flesh" of the world and has altered the destiny of our host cell forever.

Jesus continues to incarnate from within. The core of who we are and of who we are becoming has been altered forever. Deeply embedded in our lives, the Lord now redirects our personality and our destiny. He is now, and for all time, One-with-us. And we, by the grace of God, are becoming one-with-Him.

11

Hope deferred makes the heart sick, but a longing fulfilled is a tree of life.

Prov. 13:1

The experience of prayer can sometimes be discouraging, even for those who are quite disciplined at it. We wrestle time out of our busy day to finally show up for that long-promised appointment with God. We offer ourselves to the Lord, and then we spend the next 20 minutes or so in an endless variety of thoughts that we could just as easily have had while driving or doing the dishes. We come to the discouraging conclusion that not only do we not know how to pray, but neither have we the will nor motivation to lead ourselves to the place of learning. Prayer seems impossible and we feel like giving up rather than subjecting ourselves to any further discouragement. Though such an experience always appears as a failure, it is also a very normal and predictable stage towards a deeper and more truthful relationship with God.

The inability to pray as we would want to is a common experience, but there is a tendency to see this failure as conclusive, and we need to be careful to avoid this misinterpretation. The ancients referred to this despairing tendency as *acadie*, the temptation to assess your spiritual progress negatively and then to give up. Acadie, or the "noon-day devil" as it's sometimes called, is a spirit of discouragement that afflicts the soul by sapping it of its strength to persevere. Our hopes for prayer are disappointed and our heart is sickened, resulting in spiritual languor. The very thought of God becomes a burden to us.

Spiritual languor is a dis-ease of the soul that mostly affects the will. It weakens our attempts to pray, and quenches our hope of persevering in the spiritual life. The desire to pray may still be present but the power and will to do so seem absent. In the end, even the desire to pray fades.

Proverbs 13:12 recognizes that when we lose hope, we feel ill. But, curiously enough, this fact is also the surest evidence that all is not without hope. The very reason that the heart is sickened is that it recognizes the terrible loss that languor represents. And it grieves this loss. The discomfort we feel in this state is proof enough of the Holy Spirit's presence and continuing activity in the soul's desire for prayer. As St. John of the Cross observed,

> It is clear that this darkness does not come from lukewarmness
> because the very nature of lukewarmness is that it does not care,
> nor is concerned with the things of God.

In the ebb and flow of our spiritual lives, it is important to recognize how the Holy Spirit uses seasons of languor in order to help strengthen and purify our desire for God. We should not measure our spiritual life only according to times of light, warmth, joy and fruitful activity. Times of impasse, of coldness towards God, of darkness and grief at the apparent loss of contact with the Lord are also active forces in our spiritual formation.

In times of spiritual languor it is important that we avoid the temptation to jump to hasty conclusions—especially if they're based solely on our own interpretation of the experience. Faith and patience, even in the midst of apparent failure, are always our best and most fruitful recourses.

12

Restore to me the joy of your salvation and grant me a willing spirit, to sustain me.

Psalm 51:12

Acadie, or spiritual languor, is an experience that is especially common for people at the beginning stages of trying to establish a discipline of prayer in their lives. They have a desire to pray but are not able to be consistent in focusing their will in order to persevere in this desire. To feel discouragement at this stage is understandable. But people with a disciplined prayer life can also experience an erosion of their will-to-pray. For them, the reasons for spiritual languor are often mysterious, and perhaps more related to God's direct activity within their souls than to their own lack of initiative.

Matthew the Poor, a Coptic contemplative, says that one of the reasons God allows us to experience spiritual languor might be in order to curtail an over-ambitious soul. This can apply to us at any stage of our pilgrimage, whenever we are tempted to turn our spiritual hopes into spiritual goals. He suggests that such a soul might be attempting to go beyond its ability to endure, beyond that which its foundations can stand. We can sometimes ask for, or expect, spiritual experiences and knowledge beyond our present needs or capacity. When such presumptions fail us we feel discouraged. We find our spiritual reserves exhausted from having over-extended ourselves.

Spiritual languor, in this context, can actually be seen as a gift of mercy as God protects us from the spiritual pride that would result if we were to claim spiritual heights that we are not yet ready for. Weakness of the will then serves to bring the soul back to the lowly steps of a beginner. It should be welcomed as a merciful corrective that empties the soul of self-willed ambition. It also re-establishes the right order of relationship between our spiritual disciplines and our experience of God.

One of the particular dangers of a disciplined spiritual life is to presume that diligence and faithfulness to our spiritual practices are directly linked to our relationship with God, as though they somehow qualify us for the love and grace of God. If that is the case, rather than allow us to persist in such an illusion, God is obliged to deprive the soul of its own energy and will in order to challenge our faulty premises.

The discipline we apply to the pursuit of God is not the price we pay for His love and acceptance, but only a response to these. Whenever God withdraws the grace of zeal from us and the soul loses the power and energy to be disciplined in its spiritual work, the spiritual poverty that results can serve to correct a misunderstanding of the relationship that binds the soul to God.

How can we know if these correctives apply to our present state of soul? Perhaps the very questions we ask ourselves when we feel tepid in our spirits are what most reveal the presumptions of relationship that we are dealing with. Has God forsaken me? Is it because of my sin? Have I provoked God to anger by my sloth and laziness? Is my prayer no longer acceptable to Him? Each of these questions reveals a faulty premise with regards to who is in response to Whom.

It is easy to believe that, if we no longer have a will for God, God no longer has a will towards us. This is what happens when we are tempted by acadie.

13

Continue to work out your salvation with fear and trembling.
Phil. 2:11

The gift of salvation is a very easy thing to take for granted. Evangelicals are especially apt at knowing the terms of the new "contract" with God, and feeling secure enough to never have to think again about the ongoing work of their own salvation. "Fear and trembling" can seem like an odd and unnecessary disposition with which to approach God. Paul's word to the Ephesians, however, certainly presumes otherwise.

Recognizing our tendency to take our spiritual lives for granted, St. Alphonsus Liguori, an 18th-century Doctor of the Catholic Church, taught that we should pray daily for four graces that are related to "working out our salvation." The four graces that we should seek anew each day are:

- for the forgiveness of our sins
- for growth in our love for God,
- for growth in our love of prayer
- for final perseverance.

To pray for such is to recognize that any grace depends solely upon God granting it, and that we should not presume upon our possession of it. The practice of seeking these four graces will impress this upon our tendencies to think otherwise.

The forgiveness of our sins is the first grace that St. Alphonsus recommends. To seek this grace daily ensures that we are not simply resting on theological presumptions. To participate in Christ's purifying work implies a continual state of rebirth and renewal that can only come from daily seeking and then receiving forgiveness for our sins. Our weekly celebration of the Eucharist is such a time when we renew, in our experience, the assurances of God's forgiveness. It is only to the degree that we recognize our need for such renewal that we can truly celebrate the mercy offered through this gift.

The second grace we should seek daily is that of a continually growing love for God. The disposition to seek this grace comes from the recognition that we do not love God as we ought to, or even wish to. Our love for God is something that can continually increase, and to desire this is, in itself, an expression of love.

The third grace—that of a growing love of prayer—is one that comes *from*, as well as leads us *to*, the love of God. Prayer is a journey heavenward and its destination is nothing short of an eternity of loving communion with God. To pray is simply to respond to God's perpetual call within us that draws us in the direction of this union—the ultimate purpose of our creation. With this in mind, we ask for increasing grace that we would love prayer as an expression of our desire for God to dwell deeply in the temple of our lives.

The final grace that St. Alphonsus Liguori counsels us to pray for is that of "final perseverance." This grace is one that recognizes that Jesus is the Author and Finisher of our faith, and that He alone can lead us to a good end to our life. In Matt. 10:22, the Lord says that "whoever stands firm to the end will be saved." To pray for this is to recognize that we cannot presume upon our own strength or abilities to finish well in life. We know well our weakness and how feeble our faith is. In seeking such a grace, we acknowledge our dependence on God to sustain us, and we recognize that, ultimately, final perseverance is a gift from God.

This is what Jesus Himself prayed for us when He asked His Father, to "keep them by the power of Your name—the name You gave me" (John 17:11). The apostle Paul also encourages us to anticipate this grace and to be confident "that He who began a good work in you will carry it on to completion until the day of Christ Jesus" (Phil. 1:6).

These four graces appropriately reflect our daily disposition as recipients of the free gift of salvation in Christ. As we accept the wisdom of this teaching it will counter any presumptions that might otherwise take root in us. And we will grow in freedom, as we become more and more dependent on God for the working out of our salvation.

14

Then Jesus said, "What is the kingdom of God like? What shall I compare it to?"

Luke 13:18

It is difficult, if not impossible, to describe the spiritual life directly. You have to "tell it slant," allude to it, use metaphor, allegory, poetry and other imagery. Even Jesus, when speaking of the spiritual life, often seemed constrained to similes in describing the kingdom of God as "like this" or "like that."

How do you picture your own spiritual life? What metaphors do you use when interpreting your experience of God? Evelyn Underhill, in her classic book on mystical theology, refers to three of the most common symbols of the spiritual life: the Pilgrim, the Lover and the Alchemist. You might recognize your own metaphor in these.

The first symbol, the Pilgrim, describes the Abrahamic quest. It appeals to our longing to go out from the "normal world" in search of an anticipated "home" or promised land. Examples in literature include Dante's *Divine Comedy,* or John Bunyan's *Pilgrim's Progress.* In these, the soul is seen as outward bound, journeying towards an anticipated goal. Its destination, or home, is something perceived in the distance. The intuition for the Pilgrim is one that interprets the spiritual cravings of the heart as indicating the longing for a "Place."

The symbol of the Lover on the other hand identifies a different interpretation of this longing—one of "heart for heart," of the soul for its perfect mate, of love for its lover. The idea of betrothal and marriage is one of its common allegories. The spiritual temperament in this disposition is that of deep desire for an intimate and personal relationship with God. This intuition is one that understands the spiritual cravings as indicating a 'Person.'

That the imagery of human love and marriage should be enlisted as a metaphor for the spiritual life is, of course, natural. In the Song of

Songs, the bride and bridegroom can represent the progression of the soul's surrender to the embrace of Perfect Love—from attraction, to knowledge, to growing intimacy, to union. It parallels the sequence of states through which our spiritual consciousness unfolds in its progress towards intimacy.

Where the Pilgrim responds to the "seek and ye shall find" promises of Scripture, and the Lover follows the desires and passions of love, the Alchemist longs more for a transformation of the soul. He is guided by Jesus' promise, "Blessed are the pure in heart, for they shall see God." The symbol of the alchemist represents the inward search for purity—the "Magnus Opus," or "Great Work of the Soul," where the need to be born again, or regenerated, is the first necessity. Paul calls it a matter of exchanging the old man for the new.

Alchemy is the art of purification—bringing forth the latent "gold" which lies obscure in the metal, or in the self. The longing for righteousness, perfection and sanctification in the spiritual life is a response to the call to "be holy as I am holy." The intuition of the Alchemist understands the spiritual cravings as mostly indicating a "State of Soul."

These three images are of course only partial descriptions of the subjective experience of spiritual life. Which ones best represent your present experience? Consider how exploring some aspects of the other metaphors might enrich your interpretation of the spiritual life.

Of course none of these symbols are exclusive, and we perhaps all share elements from each. But they are helpful to consider as we appreciate the variety of spiritual experiences that are identified in us through such imagery.

15

The wise heart will know the proper time and procedure. For there is a proper time and procedure for every matter.

Eccl. 8:5-6

Throughout his ministry, Oswald Chambers, the author of *My Utmost for His Highest* followed a daily motto to simply "trust God and do the next thing." He was comfortable with the fact that he could not see the whole picture, and in the knowledge that the journey can just as easily be made by a thousand small steps as by a few giant leaps. This is the type of wisdom that faith inspires.

Faith rests in the knowledge that the Lord has already prepared a path for us to walk each day. If we just wait long enough, it will reveal itself. We might not know where this path is leading us. We might not even like where it's going. But there is definitely a path for each one of us to walk, and Jesus has identified it as none other than Himself—the "Way." Seeking and waiting for Jesus each day is how we come to know "the proper time and procedure for each matter."

The book of Proverbs agrees with the wisdom of patience when it comes to finding our path. In Prov. 4:26 we are encouraged to "make level paths for your feet and take only ways that are firm." There are many times when we must wait for the dust of confusion to settle before the way can be revealed to us. To start walking any sooner, on what is still rough and uncertain terrain, is seen as foolishness. Wisdom knows that it is best to wait until "the proper time and procedure" is revealed.

To wait on God, of course, is a test of our faith. It means staring into the void and feeling secure enough to do nothing about it. We are not very comfortable with uncertainties. We often panic when we don't know what to do. And in our anxiety we feel compelled to take any action rather than no action at all. But the contemplative life encourages us to give proper time for things to unfold before we act. New information will show up tomorrow that you could not possibly have known today. Your own disposition and state of soul will be different an hour from now than it is at present. *Make level paths for you feet..*

There are patterns of direction to all things in life and they will emerge in their own time. You will know which way is firm, and the proper time and procedure for every matter. And, until you do, you are counseled to wait.

16

Blessed are the poor in spirit for theirs is the kingdom of heaven.

Matt. 5:3

The assurances we hear in the Beatitudes—that the hungry will be filled, that those who mourn will be comforted, and that the meek will be victorious—can sound like "pie in the sky" being offered to those who have no other hope on earth. But to see them as invitations through which Jesus calls us and reveals to us important identifiers of the spiritual life would be a more likely interpretation.

St. Francis of Assisi certainly understood the human predicament in these terms. He knew, firsthand, how we are fundamentally incomplete, fragile and broken people. It would be easy to think that such a state of affairs is a serious problem that needs correcting. But anyone who has studied the saint's teaching knows that his description of humanity refers not only to our starting point, but to the end we must accept as well.

According to St. Francis, the most accurate theological definition of the human race is that it is made up of people who are "striken with egoistic tendencies, always tempted to affirm themselves as self-sufficient." Francis identifies this as resulting in them "abandoning themselves far too often and disfiguring the image according to which they have been fashioned."

But, according to St. Francis, there is also good news in this diagnosis. Jesus, in the Beatitudes, has proposed for us a way of conversion. He invites us to embrace our poverty—our fragile, broken and incomplete self—as not only the beginning, but also as the end of our spirituality. In order to enter into the full blessing (literally, the "happiness") of the Beatitudes we must, according to Francis, learn to both "experience and assume the radical poverty of our being." To adopt this tack will immediately challenge the direction that most of our efforts at sanctification take.

Most of us have spent years, and much psychological energy, trying to distance ourselves from the poverty of our being. Or we have tried to correct our inconsistencies on our own. We tend to see our brokenness as a temporary problem, an impediment that we hope to overcome on the road to true freedom.

But if Jesus, in the Beatitudes, is teaching us the proper disposition of blessing, then our attempts to undo the poverty of our being might actually be spiritual energy spent in the wrong direction. If Jesus is right, we should be learning instead how to accept, even to embrace, our deficiencies rather than trying to distance ourselves from them. Like it or not, they are the truth of who we presently are

The call of the Beatitudes is to a radical change of agenda from how we normally understand our spiritual direction. *This is the call*—to deeply experience and to assume as our spiritual path a growing acceptance of the incompleteness of who we are. *This is the call*—to welcome our fragility and so discover a new type of blessing that we have perhaps never known.

Jesus sees our poverty as blessed. This is reason enough to embrace the teaching of the saints in this matter.

17

Each one is tempted when, by his own evil desire, he is dragged away and enticed.

James. 1:14

To appreciate how this passage applies to spiritual direction and to the purification of our desires we need to first redeem the word "evil" from its usual associations with morality. The Greek word that James uses here is *kakos.* This word for "evil" does not necessarily describe the moral quality of something as much as the negative effect it has. What makes something evil is that it is injurious in its effect, making something worth less than it could be. In this sense, an "evil" desire is one that takes away from the spiritual potential of our better desires. Its association with sin, then, is also in the sense that it causes us to "miss the mark" or fall short of the prize.

The apostle James exhorts us to take stock of the inordinate desires that lure us away from the God-given goals that our purer desires are otherwise calling us to. Jesus' temptation in the desert, for example, was an attempt to lure Him away from the better focus of His life, i.e. to entice Him to miss the mark and fall short of the prize.

Some desires are more worthwhile than others. If we follow every one of our desires indiscriminately we will make a rabbit trail of our lives. Our lesser desires will entice us towards lesser goals, and cause us to lose sight of the noble vision we once had for ourselves. But, if we endeavour to fan the flame of our God-given desires, it will lead us to a deeper experience of relationship with the Divine "object" of our longings.

Lord, lead us not into temptation, but deliver us from worthless things.

18

Be filled with the Spirit.

Eph. 5:18

If we want to obey Paul's exhortation what exactly are we supposed to do? How does one go about becoming "filled with the Spirit?" The commandment is given to us in an imperative form and yet it calls for an action than none of us, by our own will or efforts, can hope to achieve. How are we to respond to this call? Perhaps the wisdom of the Orthodox church can help us better understand the intention of this Scripture.

For the Orthodox theologian, there are always two distinctions that one must make in interpreting Scriptures. These form the basis for the difference between *dogmatic* theology and *ascetic* theology. The first refers to what we believe Scripture is saying. The second, to what we must do in order to live in the reality of what we believe.

The Holy Spirit, as Scripture teaches us, is a deposit, or promise, that we receive at baptism. This is the *dogmatic* theology. As this statement of belief evolves towards *ascetic* theology however, we see that what is implied is that the Spirit, though present in us, must be given every opportunity to now fill us. In other words we are called to increasingly give the Spirit freedom to work in us, without hindrance, until the fullness that this passage promises is realized.

The Greek verb *pleroo* which we translate as "be filled" is in the imperative passive form. It means to "let yourself be filled." It is the Spirit who fills us, but we can provide occasion for this to happen. Orthodox theology would state that the Holy Spirit is already present within us through baptism, but that it remains a latent presence, unfelt and relatively idle until we commit to inflame this gift by kindling its fire, and by removing obstacles that would prevent it from filling our hearts and ruling our lives. Consider this distinction in light of Paul's injunction in Gal. 5:25 where both dogmatic and ascetic theology are indicated: "If we live by the Spirit, let us also walk by the Spirit." The one does not necessarily assume the other.

It is faith that transforms God's free gift into commitment and into a desire to see the promises of Scripture perfected in our actions and in our being. As we make room in our heart and life for the Holy Spirit, He in turn makes room within us for Christ. As Matta El-Maskeen, the Coptic hermit, states,

> Christ is manifested in His saints to the degree to which they can bear the fullness of the Spirit, by preparing the heart to be a comfortable home for His perpetual residence.

Consider what it means for you to surrender yourself more fully to the action of the Holy Spirit. To "be filled" means to allow your entire life—your past, present and future, your weakness and your strength, your successes and your failures, your health and your sickness—to be directed towards the fruit for which Christ died for you—an abundant life in the Spirit.

19

The disciples asked him privately, "Why couldn't we drive (the evil spirit) out?" He replied, 'This kind can come only by prayer and fasting.'

Mark 9:28-29

The Lord gives us wonderful gifts with which to serve others. But if these gifts are not vitally connected to the Giver of our gifts, we will likely fall flat on our faces in terms of our effectiveness. This is the hard lesson the disciples had to learn.

God has empowered us to influence the world for good, but let us not underestimate the inner work that is required in order for our outer works to bear their intended fruit. The type of spiritual transformation that we are meant to be agents of in this world can only come about by diligence in remaining close to God—the "prayer and fasting" that Jesus prescribes.

To be spiritually applied in this world requires that we give ourselves not only to the needs of the world around us, but also to God. We must tend to both the horizontal and vertical necessities of each. Only that which comes from God can truly serve God in this world. In order for us to be spiritually effective in our influence He must be the source of our empowerment. The disciples' failure here is an object lesson for us all to heed.

In the story that precedes this passage from Mark, Jesus has just spent the night on the Mount of Transfiguration with Peter, James and John. In His absence, the remaining disciples have been dealing with a concerned father who has brought his son, possessed by an evil spirit, in the hope of receiving healing. The disciples, though initially buoyed by their recent successes in healing and casting out demons on their own, are unable to help. They appear as fakes to the scribes and mockers who deride them. To the father who had put his faith in them, this seems to be nothing but a cruel hoax. The disciples are speechless, humiliated by their spiritual impotence and exposed as much less than their reputation among the villagers had promised.

In John 15, Jesus speaks of a branch that is severed from the vine which, now withered, is only good to be thrown away. Surely these words must be resonating in the disciples' thoughts. But Jesus' parable also provides the antidote to their ineffectiveness. *Remain in me and you will bear much fruit..*

The lesson that this failure taught the disciples is that of the importance of preparation. It's a lesson we have to learn over and over again, usually through the humbling experience of our own of failures.

Lord, why aren't we more successful in our ministry? Why do I feel so spiritually impotent? Why does the church seem so ineffective in bringing about spiritual change in the world? *This kind can only come by prayer and fasting.*

20

Do not merely listen to the word, and so deceive yourselves. Do what it says. Anyone who listens to the word but does not do what it says is like a man who looks at his face in a mirror and, after looking at himself, goes away and immediately forgets what he looks like. But the man who looks intently into the perfect law

that gives freedom, and continues to do this, not forgetting what
he has heard, but doing it—he will be blessed in what he does.

James 1:22-25

For decades I've been attracted to the vocation of a painter. I am a reasonably good amateur watercolourist. I've had exhibits, sold paintings, been affirmed by others in this and enjoy seeing my works up on the walls of friends. But the busy-ness of life and other priorities have, for many years, made it impossible to realistically call myself a practicing artist.

Whenever I visit galleries and see beautiful works that others have created, I often leave with a great sense of excitement and vision for the type of art I might be capable of producing myself, if I could only find the time. I recognize, in the joy I experience viewing the work of other artists, an invitation to find that same profound potential within myself. But that joy will never, on its own, lead me to becoming a good artist. The only way I will ever reach this aspiration is by getting down to some serious painting.

Many people feel a similar attraction to the contemplative life and practice. It represents something of the state of soul their hearts long for as they recognize their own desires in the writings of the saints, especially in the descriptions of the intimacy they enjoy with God. God has placed such a cloud of witnesses all around us, but it is important that we not confuse firsthand experience with what is secondhand. God's invitation is not to live vicariously, but to enjoy directly the experience of the Spirit that is uniquely ours. As A.W. Tozer put it, we are each called "to push into sensitive living experience into the Holy Presence of God." And more and more people, it seems, are hearing this call.

Anyone browsing the latest titles in a Christian bookstore will recognize that there is a growing interest in spirituality. As Eugene Peterson observes in his *Christ Plays In Ten Thousand Places*,

> In our times "spirituality" has become a major business for
> entrepreneurs, a recreational sport for the bored, and for others,
> whether many or few, a serious and disciplined commitment to
> live deeply and fully in relation to God.

35

Though it gives us cause to hope that a growing interest in the spiritual life will translate into spiritual fruit, this is not necessarily the case any more than an increase in people attending art galleries will produce a crop of artists. Reading book after book can give us the illusion of spiritual growth, but it will never amount to the transformation that spiritual practice offers to anyone who "does what the word says."

The desire that inflames the heart whenever we hear or read about intimacy with God must somehow translate into our own journeying in the direction of that intimacy. James' encouragement—to be doers and not only hearers of the word—certainly applies to the call to "push into sensitive living experience into the Holy Presence of God."

For those who already enjoy a regular discipline of prayer, the apostle John assures you (1Jn 2:27, below) that you are in the place of instruction whereby the Holy Spirit will continue to lead you directly into all the subtleties of this relationship. For those who are not yet able to enjoy such a regular discipline in their lives, may your longing for such be the prayer and hope that God has claimed you for this end.

> As for you, the anointing you received from him remains in you, and you do not need anyone to teach you. But as his anointing teaches you about all things and as that anointing is real, not counterfeit—just as it has taught you, remain in him.
>
> 1 John 2:27

21

> Search me, O God, and know my heart;
>   test me and know my anxious thoughts.
> See if there is any offensive way in me,
>   and lead me in the way everlasting.
>
> Psalm 139:23-24

The values of prayer are many. Anyone who practices it enjoys the assurance of Divine relationship in all aspects of their lives. It gives them hope in their petitions, a path through the uncertainties of life, and a real sense of participation with God's purposes in the world. Prayer also leads us to wisdom and self-knowledge. It is the laboratory where the subtleties of the spiritual life are closely examined, and where we can hope to discern the mysterious forces that move us to think and act as we do. Prayer is also the place of new beginnings—where life gets birthed, fresh from the Word. In so many ways prayer is a wellspring of spiritual growth. But one of the often unheralded benefits of prayer is that it also prevents certain things from growing. It is a place where bad growth is curtailed.

Growth happens imperceptibly, especially bad growth—the negative attitudes we cultivate, the prejudices we develop, the priorities we misplace, and the misinterpretations of God's will that can cause us to gradually wander from the truth. Without prayer these harmful growths go unchecked. Prayer is the place of pruning where such things are nipped in the bud. It prevents them from ever taking root in us.

In prayer we ask God to examine all aspects of our lives in order to avoid such errors. Like shining a flashlight in a dark basement we look into this corner and that one, holding all things up to God to see if there is anything that needs to be adjusted. "What do you think of this Lord? What about my relationship with so and so? What about this choice or action I made today? What about this attitude I feel growing in me? Is that ok with you? Is everything alright? Is there anything offensive in me?"

Prayer is the place where we get to re-examine and adjust the assumptions we are operating under. It is where we come to have our lives redirected as needed. To ask God daily for verification is the simple ounce of prevention that will make unnecessary the pound of cure that any wrong tangent will eventually require,.

> *Each one should be careful how he builds. For no one can lay any foundation other than the one already laid, which is Jesus Christ. If any man builds on this foundation using gold, silver, costly stones, wood, hay or straw, his work will be shown for what it is, because the Day will bring it to light. It will be revealed with fire, and the fire will test the quality of each man's work.*
>
> 1 Cor. 3:10-14

22

Godly sorrow brings repentance that leads to salvation and leaves no regret, but worldly sorrow brings death.

2 Cor. 7:10

In the *Sayings of the Desert Fathers,* there is a story of Abba Sisoes who is lying on his deathbed. He is surrounded by his disciples who see that he appears to be talking to someone. "Who are you talking to Father?," his disciples ask him. "See," he replies, "the angels have come to take me and I am asking for a little more time—more time to repent." "But you have no need to repent," his disciples say to him." "Truly" the old man replies, "I am not sure if I have even begun to repent,"

Anticipating the purity of heaven, Abba Sisoes desires more time to repent. He realizes that there are aspects of his life and of his relationship with God that he has been putting off or willfully ignoring and he knows, without a doubt, that he will soon have no further opportunity to deal with these. The heightened awareness that he is about to meet the Lord inspires a heightened desire in him for innocence and truth. And he hopes for more time to respond to the call to repentance. This could be an anxious moment if not for the promise that this type of "godly sorrow" leaves no regret.

Spiritual repentance hones us to the correct measure of heaven's gate. It chips away the excess that we would otherwise regret. The godly sorrow that becomes our prayer results from the inner workings of the Holy Spirit whose purpose it is to convince us of our sin (John 16:8). And it is to our benefit that we learn how to participate with this merciful agenda. To know our sins in the context of God's love is to be free from the illusions that otherwise make us complacent and rob us of any real incentive to be holy.

True repentance brings with it a balm that heals our souls. It has nothing to do with self-loathing, which only brings death. If our repentance is taking place in a spirit of hope, its fruit will be freedom, not guilt. St. Ignatius tells us how to discern the opposite effect of "worldly sorrow." He says that it is characteristic for a negative spirit to "afflict with sadness, to harass with anxiety and to raise obstacles based on false reasoning." If this is the effect our "worldly" repentance is having on us we can likely suspect that its origin is not in the Holy Spirit.

It is the kindness of God that leads us to true repentance (Rom. 2:4). And it is by embracing it as such that we most honour the work of the Holy Spirit within us.

> *True repentance has a joyful note to it. The ice of hard-heartedness and self-righteousness has been broken and spring has entered the heart.*
>
> *Like a spring breeze the Holy Spirit blows through the heart enabling it to weep over its sins but to rejoice in the Lord's forgiveness and grace.*
>
> *What a blessed gift repentance is!*
>
> Basilea Schlink

23

The spirit is willing, but the body is weak.

Matt. 26:41

It is a dismayingly common experience, having finally settled down to pray, to find that you are not able to do so. The mind seems to suddenly become more active than usual with a thousand concerns, all unrelated to our goal of prayer. Why is this? Is there any hope that we can ever adapt to the Spirit of stillness and become what prayer requires of us? The late psychiatrist and spiritual director Gerald May thought so, and in his book, *Addiction and Grace*, offered a physiological explanation of what takes place within us as we set out to pray.

Over the course of our lives, each one of us has established what our bodies understand as their "normal" inner disposition—a particular equilibrium that it strives to maintain. Even if the "normal" that we live with is an uncomfortable one, it is the one that we have become accustomed to and any attempt to alter this inner state is going to be met with physiological resistance. We are, in a sense, "addicted" to whatever constitutes our norm and, as Gerald May puts it, "I don't let that normality change without a struggle." He identifies the struggle involved in any attempt to transform our norms as similar to that of someone withdrawing from an addiction—in this case, an addiction to self.

> For many modern spiritual pilgrims, the simple matter of taking time for daily prayer can become a battle of will excruciatingly reminiscent of that encountered in chemical addiction. Issues of control and willpower, surrender and defeat all rage within the drama of a true spiritual warfare. Increasing numbers of us are discovering that we would rather stay the same than experience the real discomfort that becoming peaceful produces in us.

Prayer, by its very nature, encourages an altered state of reference within us. It seeks to establish a new norm. We should not underestimate the withdrawal process that such transformation entails. We have, after all, spent years establishing a "norm" for ourselves, apart from God. As Gerald Mays puts it,

> Mediating all the stimuli they receive, the cells of our brains are continually seeking equilibrium, developing patterns of adaptation that constitute what is normal. Thus the more we become accustomed to seeking spiritual satisfaction through things other than God, the more abnormal and stressful it becomes to look to God directly for these.

This logic particularly applies to the abnormal demands that the practice of prayer places on our physiology. It also explains why, at least initially, our bodies register this sudden change of inner state as discomfort. Since we are addicted to a much more active inner life, we naturally have trouble letting go of it as we attempt to enter a state of prayer. As Gerald May notes,

> If a person takes a vacation or tries to settle down to pray, the sudden removal of external stress immediately causes the body to generate less stress chemicals. The neurons, having been adapted to high levels of stress chemicals, now react as if something were wrong. They send signals, ironically, of stress to the rest of the body, trying to get things going again.

Prayer is a catalyst for transformation and, for this reason alone, we should anticipate that it will imply a struggle between the flesh and the spirit. Adapting to change will inevitably mean going through the stress of withdrawal from our old normality, until our new one is established.

24

By the seventh day God had finished the work he had been doing; so on the seventh day he rested from all his work. And God blessed the seventh day and made it holy, because on it he rested from all the work of creating that he had done.

Gen. 2:2-3

From day one of creation, God's method has been one of separating, in order to define—making distinctions between darkness and light, the waters above and waters below, the land and the sea, etc. Here too, on the seventh day, God creates an important distinction, this time between work and rest. In so doing He makes a clear separation between Himself and His work. He distinguishes action from being,

Imagine if, on the seventh day, God would have just continued adding more and more amazing feats of creation to His accolades. Imagine if the Genesis story was simply a story about God's work. It would still be pretty impressive to create a whole universe and set man and history into motion. We would still marvel at God, the Creator. The problem with this story however is that we would naturally identify God in only one mode—that of Worker-Creator. We would see Him as an active God who is forever busy creating.

Instead, Scripture makes an important distinction. *On the seventh day the Lord rested from His work.* In other words, He returned to His first identity—who He is, independent of His work.

Taking rest from work is one of the most affirming statements we can make about the work we do. "It is finished." "It is good." "It has its life and I have mine." It is also one of the most affirming statements that we can make about ourselves. "I am not my work." We stand apart, in wonderful relationship to it, but not exclusively defined by what we do.

It is good. In his famous *Practice Resurrection* lectures, Eugene Peterson speaks of the Sabbath as the place from which we get to practice and cultivate such wonder. In order to do so we need to maintain a

41

healthy sense of objectivity in relation to our work-life. If we focus too closely on what we do, on mastery and competence in our environment as the foundation of our being, we can easily lose our sense of objective wonder. "It is good" can mistakenly start to imply that "I am good."

Sabbath, then, is a time for cultivating restful objectivity in our relationship to work. It is a God-given opportunity to get rid of the idols we might've created during the week—our inordinate attachments to what we do. Both God's exhortation and His example call us to practice times of detachment—to intentionally rest from our work, just as He did from His.

25

Who shut up the sea behind doors when it burst forth from the womb, when I made the clouds its garment and wrapped it in thick darkness, when I fixed limits for it and set its doors and bars in place, when I said, 'This far you may come and no farther?

Job 38:8-11

The Lord sets limits to all things. *This far you may come and no farther.* While God calls us to grow, He also places boundaries that limit our growth. If we can accept the fact that there are God-ordained purposes to the limitations of our life we can perhaps be more open to acknowledging them and learning how work within their constraints.

Our lives are as circumscribed as the contours of the sea. If we could draw a topographical map of the shape of our gifts in terms of the present limits of our capacities, we would recognize what God sees and we would know why our grasp is often much shorter than our reach. *This far you may come and no farther.* To accept the God-set contours of our lives doesn't mean settling for mediocrity, nor does it offer divine justification for us to be underachievers, but it does allow us to consider the possibility that limitations, in themselves, are not necessarily problems to overcome on the road to self-fulfillment.

If we consider the vision we perhaps had for ourselves in our youth and compare it to the relatively less impressive life we have since lived, we might feel like we've failed in achieving our potential, or that we've been short-changed in life. But could it be that God has directed you as much by your limitations as by your potential? Could it be that you are exactly where you are because God didn't give you the capacity to be anywhere else at this time? And could it be that He sees the limitations of your life more as an opportunity than as an impediment? In directing our lives God is able to use the things we lack as much as the things we have.

Perhaps the Lord has given you a measure of talent, but no more. What is His purpose in this limitation? Perhaps God has given you these few resources to work with, but no more. What is His purpose in this limitation? Perhaps God has given you some opportunities for ministry, but no more. What is the purpose in this limitation? Or perhaps the Lord has given you insight, allowed you to understand this much truth, and no more. What is the purpose of this limitation?

God establishes limits, and Christian theology assumes that freedom is realized through and in relation to such purposeful constraints. It is the narrowness of the river banks, after all, that gives strength to the river.

26

I am my Beloved's and He is mine.

Song of Solomon 2:16

Love is possessive, in the best sense of the word. It desires, recognizes and assures us that we belong to the One who loves us, and that the One we love also belongs to us. But this status of "belonging" is not something that we can ever secure for ourselves. It must be given freely by the other person. That is why love, by its very nature, is always precarious.

The word "precarious" is curiously rooted in the same Old Latin word from which we derive the word prayer. It refers to the risk involved when something depends wholly upon the will of another. In other words, to rest in the statement "I am loved by you" means to be in a place of precarious vulnerability, requiring utmost trust of the other person. We need to understand how this applies to our relationship with God, as well as to one another, if we are to appreciate the risk and responsibility that free love entails.

It is natural that experiences of fear and vulnerability often accompany the growing edge of love. As we put our lives on the altar of its flame, love demands that we trust the precarious power we have given the other person. This is also the risk that God has taken in granting His creatures the freedom to love Him or not. And it's the risk that any believer must take in trusting that God's love for us is greater than our fears would imply. The confident assurance expressed in the statement "I am my beloved and He is mine" represents the victory of such trust over our fears.

Love leads us in the direction of trust through a slow process of transformation as we come to recognize the many layers of fear and insecurities that need to be overcome on the road to "possessing" it. We "possess" love only insofar as we receive it in trust. One of the oldest definitions of the word *possess* is of something that we "hold, occupy, or reside in." Resting in love, then, means to reside, or feel at home, in the assurance that we truly belong there.

27

It may be that the LORD will see my distress and repay me with good for the cursing I am receiving today.

2 Sam. 16:12

The story of Shimei, openly cursing David, and of the king's unexpected response (2 Sam.16:5-14) is one that anyone who is familiar with suffering, with temptation, or who has lived long in a critical environment can certainly learn from. If you haven't read the story in a while here's how it goes...

King David has just been usurped by his renegade son, Absalom, who is now on his way to Jerusalem to assume his father's throne. David is fleeing the city with his officials. As they reach the outskirts of Jerusalem they are met by Shimei, of the same clan as Saul, who boldly curses the king and his entourage, pelting them with stones as they march by. "Get out, get out, you man of blood, you scoundrel!," he heckles from the roadside. "The LORD has repaid you for all the blood you shed in the household of Saul, in whose place you have reigned. The LORD has handed the kingdom over to your son Absalom. You have come to ruin because you are a man of blood!"

Abishai, one of the King's commanders says to David, "Why should this dead dog curse my lord the king? Let me go over and cut off his head." David's response is not one you would expect from someone who is used to absolute authority. And the way he interprets this situation is both surprising as well as a lesson for any of us who need forbearance in dealing with a sustained negative circumstance.

David tells his commander not to interfere—to let Shimei continue with his curses saying, "If he is cursing because the LORD said to him, 'Curse David,' who can ask, 'Why do you do this?' Let him curse, for the LORD has told him to." He then adds, "It may be that the LORD will see my distress and repay me with good for the cursing I am receiving today." And so David continues along the road with Shimei following the whole way along a hillside "cursing as he went and throwing stones at him and showering him with dirt (v. 13)."

We too know such voices in life that curse and shower us with dirt along the way. Perhaps it's in the form of difficult trials that can't be avoided, or perhaps it's an inner voice that curses us throughout our day. Or it might be a person who always seems critical towards us. There are many irritants that seem to accompany us our whole life and we wish we could somehow shut them up. The thought that these voices might actually be messengers from God is not necessarily the first interpretation that comes to mind.

But David, in one of his nobler moments, believes this to be the case. He is a man, humbled by circumstances, who is prepared to believe that God's blessing might mysteriously be present in the painful situation that now afflicts him. He even hopes that the Lord might have pity on him, and repay him with good for the suffering he endures today.

The chapter ends with an understandable statement, "The king and all the people with him arrived at their destination exhausted." We know how such trials of the spirit can harangue us to the point of exhaustion. But the verse continues, "and there he refreshed himself."

If there is a lesson for us in David's example it is this—that we not be too quick to presume the origin or purpose of the negative spirits in our life. If they are there because God has permitted them, who can say "Why do you do this?" As we bear, in faith, the things that can't be changed in our lives, perhaps our hope might be like David's—that the Lord will see our distress and repay us with good for the things we suffer today.

28

It is fine to be zealous, provided the purpose is good, and to be so always and not just when I am with you.

Gal. 4:18

There is a bit of a misnomer in the term "spiritual direction," especially as it applies to the helper who is often called a "spiritual director." It would be easy to think that a spiritual director is someone who is somehow going to make you grow spiritually. But spiritual direction is more something that *you* do in between the times of outside guidance. It's much more accurate to consider the term "spiritual direction" as referring to the path or momentum that, at times, we are in. At other times, it might be quite honest to say that we are without spiritual direction—that we are wandering.

In the Scripture above, Paul tells us to make sure that we maintain our spiritual direction, especially during the in-between times, when we are not at church, or with a mentor, or at a prayer group. It means doing whatever we can to keep our day-to-day lives pointed towards growth in the Lord and not letting ourselves get side-tracked from this direction. To learn how to remain zealous and focused in a sustained response to God's invitation is the art of the spiritual life. Once this response is in place in our lives, we can truly say that we are living in the momentum of spiritual direction. Spiritual guidance can then become a helpful ally to your journey.

It takes a lot of energy to get a ship moving but, once it is cutting through the water, a slight adjustment of the rudder is enough to guide it all the way to port. In the same way, a spiritual director, more than being the wind in your sails, is someone who helps you consider the adjustments to your rudder that will help you stay on course. The presumption, however, is that your life is already in motion towards God, or at least, that that is what you are desiring.

Ultimately every believer is invited to find, for themselves, the motivation of love that will encourage them in their daily walk towards God. Neither spiritual directors, mentors, books, prayer partners, nor the church can be any more than outside influences in this. As the folk song goes,

> "You've got to walk that lonesome valley.
> You've got to walk it on your own.
> Nobody else can walk it for you.
> You've got to walk it on your own."

This necessary "aloneness" is part of the incredible privilege that comes from being uniquely loved by a God who calls us into personal relationship.

29

Here is a trustworthy saying: If we died with him, we will also live with him.

2 Tim. 2:11

Consider this hypothetical, alternative version of the Lord's Supper: The Lord Jesus, on the night He was betrayed, sat at table with His disciples and there suddenly appeared on the table a golden crown. Jesus lifted up the crown, and when He had given thanks, He passed it among his disciples saying, "This is my crown, which is for you. Take it and put it on, each one of you. Do this in remembrance of me. For whenever you place this crown on your head, you proclaim the Lord's victory until He comes."

Why didn't Jesus choose this as a sign of remembrance for us rather than bread and wine? Why not call us to remember Him with a symbol of His ultimate victory instead of the graphic reminders of His suffering and death on a cross? Wouldn't a celebration of His resurrection be enough to inspire hope in the worst of our circumstances?

At a recent Imago Dei fellowship we explored, at a very personal level, the nature of lost things in life—lost health, lost relationships, lost hope, lost opportunities. It is so disappointing when our experience of life falls short of the hopes we had for ourselves or for others. We feel robbed, short-changed, somehow singled-out by this diminishment of our expectations. And it seems especially unfair when we can readily think of scores of people who do not suffer similar loses.

Where is God when our circumstances end up being so much less than we conceived possible? Where is Jesus when we are feeling disappointed about our lives? Where is the hope that comes from His victory when it doesn't seem to apply to us? Our ritual of remembrance, the bread and wine of Eucharist, answers us in those times in exactly the same way as when we are feeling on top of the world—He is right here with us.

Jesus invites us to gather—to form an intimate relationship with Him—around a symbol that commemorates His place of greatest loss. The broken Body and poured Blood that these elements represent invite us to come and fellowship with Jesus at the point of His greatest sense of bankruptcy, His ultimate aloneness, and the apparent loss of all His life opportunities. It is from such places of poverty that the Lord calls us to draw realistic hope. *Take and eat, every one of you.* It is especially in such places of loss that Jesus stands with us.

No other religion celebrates, in the way we do, the signs of their leader's vulnerability. Jesus invites us to do just that. No other God personally demonstrates grace in the places where life appears most diminished. Jesus does just that. That the Lord would invite us to fellowship with Him by commemorating the very symbols of His own death, and would assure us that, even there, He stands victoriously with us, is what makes Christianity the precious pearl that it is.

> *Here is a trustworthy saying: If we died with him, we will also live with him.*
>
> 2 Tim. 2:11

30

Isaac's servants dug in the valley and discovered a well of fresh water there. But the herdsmen of Gerar quarreled with Isaac's herdsmen and said, "The water is ours!" So he named the well

Esek, because they disputed with him. Then they dug another well, but they quarreled over that one also; so he named it Sitnah. He moved on from there and dug another well, and no one quarreled over it. He named it Rehoboth, saying, "Now the LORD has given us room and we will flourish in the land."

Gen. 26:19-22

There are places in life where we belong and other places where we don't. It takes wisdom to know the difference and courage to move accordingly. Sometimes we have no choice but to learn to adapt to a situation that is ill-fitting. Other times God might use us to transform an environment into something that is more suitable for ourselves, and for others. But often, when we discern that a situation is not a good fit for us, we are simply called to move on until we find rest in a more hospitable landscape. This was certainly Isaac's experience of God's leading. Jesus taught His disciples a similar means of discernment on another occasion.

In Matt. 10:11-14, Jesus sends His disciples to the surrounding villages to minister wherever they can. The Lord tells them, as they go from place to place, that they are to stay "wherever their peace rests." If they find no peace in a town they are to take this as an obvious directive to move on. In other words, Jesus tells them that one of the ways they will discern God's direction in their pilgrimage is by the spirit of hospitality they encounter along their way.

This is similar to our passage from Genesis. Isaac's servants are sent to dig wells in a new land. It takes three attempts before they are finally able to stake a claim. In the first two attempts they are met with resistance from competing herdsmen who quarrel with the servants about ownership of the property. The third hole, however, is dug without incident. Isaac gave names to each of these three wells and the names he chose for them can give us insight into a strategy of spiritual direction that might, on occasion, be worth considering.

Isaac named the first well Esek, a word which means "dispute," and then left it unfinished. The second well he named Sitnah, meaning "opposition," and again he left it in order to continue searching for God's leading. Isaac recognized the inhospitality of these first two attempts, named them as such, and then moved on. The third well, the place where his peace

49

finally rested, he named Rehoboth, which means "room." In his great joy at having finally found a place of rest and stability he stated confidently, "Now the Lord has given us room and we will flourish in the land." Isaac recognized the hospitality of this environment as a confirmation of God's direction and as a promise of His further blessing.

These passages certainly resonate with some basic principles of spiritual direction. The presence of God's peace or disquiet within us can often be indicators of whether we belong somewhere or not, and there is wisdom in heeding the insights our experience offers us in these matters. Our souls can sense when we are trying to put a square peg into a round hole, and we should be careful that we are not stubbornly trying to force ourselves into situations we weren't made for.

Jesus told His disciples that they should remain in the places where their peace rests. Where are those places in your life, or on your horizons at present? Are you in-between wells, meeting with opposition or disputes that are forcing you to continue searching for where you belong? What are the places or conditions of hospitality to which God is presently inviting you to take rest? Where is the Lord giving you "room to flourish?" It seems an important matter in spiritual direction that we be attentive to signs of hospitality and wait for peace to be firmly established, as we discern our way with God.

31

See, I have given you this land.

Deut. 1:8

There is no greater security than to know that you are where you are because the Lord has led you there. After a decision has been made, the most satisfying state to be in is to be able to say, with some degree of confidence, that this is the house, the job, the person, the purchase, or the course of action, etc. that I believe God has led me to. Taking the time to ensure a good discernment process in charting our spiritual direction will help free us from the self-doubt and fear that often accompany any major decisions in life.

But how does one go about discerning God's will in order to enjoy such confidence in the choices we make? Thomas Green, a contemporary Jesuit spiritual director, has much to say about this in his book, *Weeds Among the Wheat*. Green stresses that, as spiritually mature men or women, we are responsible to judge and discriminate between authentic and inauthentic "voices" of God as we discern our way. The apostle John agrees, "Dear friends, do not believe every spirit, but test the spirits to see whether they are from God (1John 4 :1)."

Discernment, like prayer, is something that can only be learned by exercising it. As we practice the art of seeking God's will for our decisions, we will come to recognize more and more the Divine promptings by which the Lord leads His sheep. The perfecting of this art will also be for the purification of our souls as what usually complicates our discernment is our entanglement with self-love and our inordinate attachments to security, control or significance.

Green lists three qualities of heart that are essential dispositions for anyone who seeks to discern the will of God. The first one is humility.

> We must be humble simply because faith situations are always obscure, and our discernment is always impeded to some extent by our own sinfulness.

Throughout the process of discernment the soul should always let itself be tempered by healthy self-doubt and by an openness to be guided by the Lord through others.

The second essential quality is courage. Discernment is not a substitute for faith; it is a way of choosing how to act in faith. The only way we will ever tell if our process of discernment is accurate or needs adjustments is by acting, in faith, on what we sense God telling us. Green writes,

> Faith gives us the courage to risk. The healthy self-doubt that comes from humility does not lead to timidity, or paralysis but, in the discerning heart, to the courage to risk. We might be mis-taken, but the Lord does not ask us to always be right. He asks us to act in faith, always true to the best understanding of His will that we can attain. Both a subjective certainty of having discerned God's will, as well as an objective uncertainty of where the Lord is leading us can co-exist.

And finally, Green identifies the disposition of peace as the most confidence-establishing quality we can have, "The Lord always speaks in peace. Turmoil, anxiety and restlessness are never signs of His voice since they are forms of desolation."

The process of discerning the particular ways that God guides us in our lives will help attune us to the Shepherd's voice that leads us. And, to the degree that we have done our best to discern God's direction for us, and are prepared to act in faith that this course of action "seems right unto the Spirit," we will enjoy confidence that the Lord is not only leading us, but also delighting in watching His purposes unfold in our lives.

32

You must be born again.

John 3:7

One of the most oft-quoted phrases of St. Francis of Assisi is what he is reported to have said to his friars towards the end of his life, "Let us begin again, for up to now we have done nothing." Francis understood the importance of constant renewal as the key to sustained spiritual growth. To live in faith that such a state of renewal is always possible is to live in the perennial wellspring of hope.

The wish to start over again is something that runs deep in our psyche. Whether it's the recognition of our need for forgiveness, or for a simple change of mood; whether it's the realization that we're on a dead-end path, or that we've just gotten up out of the wrong side of the bed, the desire for a new beginning is something we naturally wish for whenever we feel stuck where we don't want to be. Life's frequent messes reveal to us how badly we need a restart button, and Jesus gives us hope that such an option is always available to us.

The most direct way to begin anew in life is, of course, through prayer. Prayer helps us get out from under the chains that we're stuck in. It's where we get to recover the fresh faith and vision that allows us to make a new start. Like the familiar rite of baptism, it is a process whereby daily, even hourly, we have opportunity to bury our old life and rise up again in newness of spirit.

By continually exchanging what is dead and decaying for what is fresh and new, prayer keeps us in a state of sustained spiritual growth. It's a process as natural as pruning dead branches off a tree, or of turning our old banana peels into rich compost. In daily prayer, as we exchange old life for new, the Lord works to keep our spirits fresh and fruitful.

33

I press on toward the goal to win the prize for which God has called me heavenward in Christ Jesus.

Phil. 3:14

I've played the flute for over 30 years. When I reflect on what has essentially made me a musician today I would attribute it to something that applies to all progress in life, including spiritual growth—the profound desire for more than what is.

Like the topic of God, music has always been a love attraction in my life. It would never have been enough for me to simply listen to music. To limit my involvement to reading *about* music would not have sufficed either. Getting to know other musicians and hearing them perform, far from satisfying my attraction, always inflamed my heart with an even greater desire to do what they do. I wanted nothing short of being at-one with this beautiful art. And so I picked up a flute and starting learning the basic mechanics of making music.

It only takes a year or so to develop enough proficiency on an instrument to play music at a novice level. But that was certainly not enough to satisfy the desire that drove my passions. As a result, I spent more and more time perfecting this craft. But the more I progressed as a musician, the more aware I also became of the technical challenges that were obstacles to the freedom I sought. I grew in greater sensitivity to all the imperfections in my tone, rhythm, phrasing and articulation. The more free I desired to be, the more I became aware of the many impediments to that freedom.

I mention all this because the pursuit of freedom is certainly not limited to music-making. We seek it in all things. And the more precisely we envision that freedom, the more aware we become of the obstacles to that state that exist within us.

A long obedience to the demands of art has allowed me today to enjoy a wonderful degree of freedom in music-making. Looking back, I see how the simple desire for more-than-what-is has always been the main catalyst for growth. And I suspect that similar dynamics apply to my relationship with God.

We should not be surprised that the more we seek spiritual truth, the more precisely we will encounter obstacles to what we seek. But we can also anticipate that the desire-for-more that God places in our hearts will be the likely means by which all our obstacles to freedom will be overcome.

34

"I have found in David, son of Jesse, a man after my own heart; he will do everything I want him to do."

Acts 13:22

Imagine having that said about you.—the Lord identifying and affirming you as someone who is after His own heart. To know that God sees you as someone who will do everything He wants you to do must be one of the highest affirmations we could ever hope for. And perhaps being such a man or woman is not as idealistic a goal as we might think. After all, David did it.

We know enough about David to question what exactly God might mean in saying that David will do everything He wants him to do. What about Bathsheba? What about his parenting skills? What about all the violence and bloodshed that marked his life? What exactly does it look like, from the Lord's perspective, for a man or woman to be "after God's own heart?" It certainly can't be something that presumes a perfect life.

The phrase, "after God's own heart" implies someone who has taken aim towards the heart of God's will. But in this case, unlike an arrow that is trying to find its mark, it is the target itself that serves to keep the arrow focused. For David, it was the bulls-eye of God's heart that worked to steady his aim whenever he wobbled. This was the corrective that kept returning him—by an often circuitous route through valleys of error, contrition and restitution—to the path of his first love.

This premise of David's life was what St. Ignatius would call our foundation principle. It is the reset button that keeps returning us back to our life's default settings. Even when he strayed, David's ultimate goal in life ensured that it would not be for long. Such was the Lord's confidence in this man's objectives that He could easily say, without qualification, that His servant will ultimately do "everything I want him to do."

The life-quality that God affirms in David is that of inevitable obedience. The Lord knows that His servant will ultimately do all that God has willed for his life. As Paul would affirm in Rom. 14:4, "he will stand because the Lord is able to make him stand." How might this same assurance apply to us? Is God perhaps much more confident of our obedience than we are? When we see our path as wandering, intermittent, or backsliding, does the Lord rest in the knowledge of our eventual obedience to everything He wants us to do?

The fact that the Lord recognizes that we are people on pilgrimage seems to be enough to assure Him of our inevitable arrival. Looking back, we will likely be able to see how we too, in setting our ultimate aim after God's own heart, have done everything the Lord wanted us to do.

35

You always resist the Holy Spirit!

Acts 7:51

It was Stephen, the church's first martyr, who addressed these words to the angry Sanhedrin mob who were about to stone him. It is easy to see how such an accusation rang true for those unbelievers. But there is something about this statement that I too find uncomfortable. In many subtle ways, I too resist the Holy Spirit, especially when I am being drawn towards the awesome intimacy of a true encounter with God.

In her book, *Spiritual Direction: Beyond the Beginnings,* Janet Ruffing elaborates on the many ways we have of slowing down the process of intimate encounter with God. Something in us resists deeper experiences of God, especially in prayer, because we often feel overwhelmed or out of control in the face of the Lord's initiative. Ruffing writes,

People frequently move away from God's inbreak into their lives because something about the experience frightens them. This something might be the surprise of God's initiation in the relationship, the intensity of God's presence, the intensity of their own response to this, a perceived threat to self-image, a change in the way prayer is experienced, or a sense that unpleasant or undesirable consequences will follow.

Resistance to prayer often manifests itself in the all too common experience of being unable to find the time to pray. We conveniently become too busy. If that is not plausible, we find other ways of avoiding close encounters of the direct kind. Even when we do make ourselves available for prayer, we often sabotage our intentions. We busy ourselves with countless mental preoccupations instead of communicating with God as we had intended.

Another way we resist the immediacy of God's initiative in prayer is by simply resorting to our safer, more familiar methods of prayer. We try to control the experience by using some self-directed means of prayer regardless of what the Lord might be doing. As Ruffing puts it, "One can easily go through the motions in prayer without ever making themselves available to God."

Resistance usually happens unconsciously so there's not much we can do about it until, by God's grace, it becomes conscious to us. The particular issues of fear and distrust that cause us to pull back from God are deeper than most of us have immediate access to. But, for those who sincerely desire close encounter with God, there is good news—the Lord is not thwarted by our tactics.

God understands, and has already factored in our still-developing capacities for intimacy. He is much more persistent in luring us into real relationship than our responses would ever warrant. Despite our many forms of creative resistance, the Lord is determined to ultimately meet us in the awesome intimacy of love. In the midst of our ambivalence, He patiently awaits us.

We are either in the process of resisting God's truth or in the process of being shaped and molded by it.

Charles F. Stanley

36

So don't be afraid; you are worth more than many sparrows.

Matt. 10:30

Most of you will remember what it was like as a kid (or perhaps even now) to walk into a dark room or basement. You can't see a thing and yet the blindness seems to cause your imagination to become more vivid and wildly creative than normal. In the darkness, all things seem possible, even the fantastic—monsters, giant spiders, a hand reaching up to touch you from behind. Fear mounts with every step. Your heart beats faster. Your spine tingles as all your senses are piqued for the irrational threat that you're sure is gathering all around you. But, as usual, nothing happens.

Odd isn't it, how darkness can produce such a heightened sense of negative anticipation in us. In the absence of information, we often tend to project our deepest fears. We fill the void with imaginary worst-case scenarios and we respond, and sometimes even act, according to the fears we project.

Lack of certainty about our future can also create a similar response in us. When we're not sure what lies ahead, our propensity for fear seems heightened. Curious isn't it? Why do we find it so hard to believe that what we don't know, won't hurt us? Why aren't we more disposed to anticipate good from the hand of the unknown?

The satirist, Mark Twain, once wrote, "I have been troubled by many threats and dangers in my life. And some of them actually happened!" Mr. Twain identifies with the curious bent we all have for living our lives in a fearful-future tense.

It would seem that a big part of the Holy Spirit's ministry with us is trying to convince us that we really don't need to fear things as much as we think we do. Jesus often settled the anxieties of His own disciples' fears with the authoritative words, "Peace be with you." In many ways the Lord continues to minister similar assurances to us.

> "Are not two sparrows sold for a penny? Yet not one of them will
> fall to the ground apart from the will of your Father. And even the

very hairs of your head are all numbered. So don't be afraid; you are worth more than many sparrows." (Matt. 10:29-31)

If the Lord is to minister His peace deeply within us we will have to also let Him deal with our irrational fears. Faith—the intentional choice to not be afraid—is the option He commands. Let us put this option into practice as part of our daily act of obedience.

37

With God all things as possible.

Matt. 19:26

Like any living language, English is always having to come up with fresh words as new discoveries or conditions arise for which its present vocabulary is not adequate. Such a new word that offers wonderful insight for spiritual direction is *pluripotential*. It is a word that originates in the field of stem cell research, but it also expresses a phenomenon that Christians have long associated with prayer—that the closer you are to God's creative hand, the more life-possibilities there seem to be.

In the miracle of embryonic growth, scientists know that cells, up to the seventh day after fertilization, have not yet differentiated. They have the potential to develop into any number of possible organs, tissues, bone or blood cells. In other words, each stem cell can evolve into a more specialized cell, such as a muscle cell, a red blood cell, or a brain cell. This is what is called their "pluripotentiality." From the humble origins of fresh new life, it does seem that all things are truly possible.

This truth is something that mystics have also observed regarding the wellspring of life they have discovered through the Holy Spirit. Through the consistent practice of prayer they have been taught how to return to a place where they are able to continually "re-originate" with God, and in so doing, have discovered this wellspring to be a place of pluripotentiality.

There is of course much controversy surrounding the ethics of stem cell research but the discovery of this phenomenon does shed a helpful light on an important principle of growth that seems to apply to all of creation, including the spiritual life—that the longer you can remain in the state of pre-conclusive definition, the more options exist for creative direction.

As we learn to dwell nearer to the Spirit's origin within us—our spiritual "stem"—we too can expect to discover something of the endless creative possibilities the Lord has for us—the pluripotentiality that comes from the place of perpetually new beginnings.

> *"There lives the dearest freshness deep down things."*
>
> —Gerard Manley Hopkins

38

For those God foreknew he also predestined to be conformed to the likeness of his Son.

Rom. 8:29

In 1962, the French and British designers of the Concorde unveiled their superspeed jet to the world. Within months of this unveiling Russian scientists, who had also been working on an aircraft that would surpass all previous speed records, showcased their model as well. To the surprise of many (and to the suspicions of others) the Russian model looked very similar to the French/British Concorde, with its sleek body and characteristic down-turned nose. But engineers from both nations knew the reason for this similarity in design. It wasn't because of some intrigue of espionage and stolen plans. It was the unseen laws of aerodynamics that dictated the shape of both these jets. If you want to design a plane that will overcome the resistance of aerodynamics in order to travel at more than 1,400mph you will, by necessity, have to conform to the familiar shape of the Concorde. The air is what will ultimately dictates the shape one must take to travel through it.

In the same way, there is a particular shape that prayer requires from us in order to "travel" through it. There are laws of spirit-dynamics that we must conform to if we want to enter the atmosphere of prayer. Jesus once used the metaphor of passing through the eye of a needle for those who would seek to enter the kingdom of heaven. Not every shape is capable of passing through such a particular opening. But those who, through the grace of the Holy Spirit, continue to seek passage towards God will gradually find themselves conformed to the shape of Christ—the humility and righteousness that this particular gate requires.

Our regular practice of prayer is the most direct sculptor of our spiritual formation. The very nature of the Divine-human relationship that it represents forces us to become smaller, more humble, more receptive in order to be rightly related to its summons.

To pray "according to the Spirit," we must learn to let go of our own design preferences in favour of the demands the spiritual environment we wish to enter will inevitably place on us. As we assume the shape dictated by the Creator's hands we will be transformed into that which conforms perfectly with what we were ultimately designed for—relationship, in form and essence, with God. Like thread that has been brought to a fine point in order to fit through the eye of a needle, prayer and the life of faith fit us more and more perfectly for heaven's gate.

39

For the word of God is living and active. Sharper than any double edged sword, it penetrates even to dividing soul and spirit.

Heb. 4:12

The desert hermit, Carlo Carretto, refers to the Bible as a book that "marries heaven and earth." In his *Joyful Exiles,* James Houston similarly says,

> The Holy Scriptures constitute the ladder of communication between earth and heaven on which there constantly ascend and descend the heavenly messengers sent out to help lift up our hearts and minds to God in spiritual communion with Him.

It would seem that, for those who have eyes to see and ears to hear, the Word of God is a very active environment. But for most of us, our hearts are not always as open to the same expectations as our theology might be. We easily lose the connection between heaven and earth that Scripture promises us, and our enthusiasm for the Bible can wax and wane accordingly.

There is a particular way that people who begin to discover God through contemplative prayer experience this waning as the Lord changes their relationship to reading the Scriptures. At first, this reorientation can be quite disconcerting as we begin to notice a weariness, or even an aversion come over us with regards to Scripture reading. It is not uncommon, for instance, to hear someone in spiritual direction say, "I used to read three chapters of the Bible faithfully each day, and now I don't even feel like opening it. What's happening to my faith?"

As we grow in a more direct intimacy with God through contemplative prayer we should not be surprised that this will as well imply a new relationship to other aspects of our faith—to worship, to the church, to our understanding of evangelism and mission, and to the way we approach Scripture reading. In light of the new reality of God's active presence that such prayer introduces us to, the Holy Spirit will likely call us to re-examine many other aspects of our faith as well.

Correctives often need to be applied to years of self-directed spirituality and to all our well-meant efforts that might not have had their origins in the Spirit's promptings. The order gets turned around as we recognize, more and more, that God alone is the Author and Finisher of our faith. As a necessary part of our maturing process, the Lord weans us from our self-directed ways, often by first taking away the satisfaction that we used to feel according to the presumptions of our old approach. He does so in order to lead us toward a more "received" relationship—one that is closer to truth than the perception that we, in any way, apprehend God through our own initiatives. This more profound integrity then brings a much deeper satisfaction to the soul, and to the Lord.

As it applies to Scripture, a contemplative re-orientation will invite us to a more Spirit-related form of reading—one whose objective is not primarily understanding, but communion with God. This shift in purpose might require us to read more slowly, perhaps going over a passage or verse a few times rather than simply skimming over it with our mind. As we learn to "feel" our way through a passage, we will detect signs of God's presence within us that confirm His active presence in the Word.

Recognizing the living nature of God's Word represents a different form of knowledge that ultimately transforms the act of reading into yet one more place of intimate communion with our Lord. We will discover the same presence of God that we have come to know through prayer, now revealed afresh through the Spirit-accompanied reading of Scripture. And, like the double-edged sword that it promises to be, the living Word of God will penetrate us deeply, creating a clearer distinction between the initiatives of our own spirit, and those of the Lord's active presence in our soul.

40

God said to Moses, "I am who I am. This is what you are to say to the Israelites: 'I AM has sent me to you.'"

Ex. 3:14

Thomas Keating, in his book, *Open Heart, Open Mind,* recommends the use of a sacred word to be repeated in our prayer time as a way of centering our thoughts on God. I've never been personally attracted to the idea of a mantra as it seems much less natural than the Father-child relationship I wish to foster with God. But I feel, nonetheless, that the Holy Spirit has evolved a sacred word in my prayer time. I don't know how transferable this is but perhaps my experience might help identify a similar movement of Spirit in you.

A few years ago I started noticing a deep response in my soul to the recognition of God's presence in my prayer. It was inexpressible at first but, as I became more familiar with this response of the heart, I started noticing words beginning to form as an articulated expression of this spirit. As they welled up in response to God, I eventually identified them as the beginning of a statement: 'You are.'

What was progressively forming in me seemed to be a spontaneous expression of praise and I naturally expected more to follow. Careful not to manipulate its evolution, I would wait in anticipation for the adverb that I thought would naturally follow this seemingly incomplete phrase. What would it be? "You are....beautiful?" "You are....gracious?" "You are.....Lord?" What was it that my soul was wanting to say to God in the recognition of His presence?

But nothing more developed. The phrase, to this very day, simply stops at "You are." I have since had time to reflect on this utterance and have come to appreciate the wonderful completeness of this sentence. The two words, "You are," simply recognize the profound fact that God *is*. They acknowledge His presence and bring assurance that this fact is sufficient enough a foundation of truth for everything else in my life.

But there is more. In further reflection on this extremely short prayer I came to recognize how the words, "You are," are, in fact, the reflex response to God's own declaration of who He is. They are an acknowledgment of the very Name by which the Lord identified Himself to Moses—"I AM." My spirit, in addressing God as "You are," is simply responding to the Lord's own self-declaration.

This could well be an experience that is unique to me, but perhaps the Holy Spirit is welling up a similar prayer response within you. If so, the advice from my experience would be to give it time to freely evolve into the Spirit-created gift of your soul's own response to the Lord's nearness.

41

For them I sanctify myself, that they too may be truly sanctified.
John 17:19

What the world needs from Christians, more than anything else, is first-hand wisdom concerning the nature of our experience in God. In his letter to the Romans, Paul tells us that the world actually "groans" for such sons and daughters to be revealed (Rom. 8:19). Our personal spiritual growth then, is something that creation both needs and longs for, and we will serve it best by our becoming what most reveals the Lord's work within us.

The desert hermit Carlo Carretto reminds us of this—that as we seek God personally, we do so not only for our own benefit, but also for the sake of others.

> Do not be in a hurry to leave your place of prayer. Do not become obsessed with time. Enjoy that peace as much as you can. It will begin to shine like a light in your face. And that will be the light your friends will be needing when you return to them. Evangelism consists in passing on that light, not the hollow sound of your own words.

For the sake of those we love, we press on in our pursuit of God. And, from the wellspring of our daily re-acquaintance with the Living Waters, we invite and encourage those around us to seek the same. The people who are able to most effectively extend this invitation are those who are most faithful in responding to this invitation themselves. They carry, within their very countenance, the attractive news of God's living "presence."

But, like God's gift of manna, the spiritual life is something that must be sought afresh each day if it is to truly feed souls—our own and those of others—in an immediate way. Carretto speaks of the winsomeness of such fresh experiences of God.

> Only the person who truly contemplates the face of God can effectively say to his brother or sister: come and see, and understand for yourself how sublime He is. To lead others to contemplation: this is the soul of evangelism. Come and see, come and try for yourself, come and experience, come with me to the holy mountain.

Ensuring that the light of Jesus is a living reality within us is the one indispensable condition on which our ability to shed light on someone else depends. Like Jesus, for the sake of those we love, we sanctify ourselves. And, in faith, we trust the mysterious and attractive operations of God's light to do the rest.

42

It is good to grasp the one
and not let go of the other.
The man who fears God will avoid all extremes.

Eccl. 7:18

E verywhere we look we see signs of tension between nations, ideologies, people and purposes. It's hard to know where to position yourself in relation to many of our contemporary cultural and global issues. And it's easy to feel that to not have a firm position on any given issue is a sign of irresponsibility, or worse, apathy. It's not a very comfortable place to be. But, for peacemakers it is often a necessary one.

One can easily get rid of the tension inherent in any complex issue by simply adopting one extreme position or another. In other words we grasp one side, while letting go of the other. But the writer of Ecclesiastes tells us that we should avoid such easy options. And so does Jesus. To bear the cross of Christ means learning to live in that very place of tension where opposites meet.

In his book, *Hope Against Darkness,* the Franciscan priest Richard Rohr observes how the greatest souls around us seem to be those who have the capacity for holding opposites together in their lives. He writes,

> By temperament, most of us prefer one side to the other. Holding to one side or another frees us from anxiety. Only a few dare to hold the irresolvable tension in the middle.

But to be cross-bearing as a Christian means exactly that—to put yourself in the "middle" without letting go of either party in order to bear, in your body, the dilemmas of the world. It is a call to stand in the gap between opposing sides of every issue—between nations, between people and their sin, between wisdom and folly, between power and weakness. It means learning how to bear vulnerability, nakedness, exposure and even failure in our body just as Jesus did, so that a bridge between the polarities might be encouraged and, eventually, formed.

The choice to willfully bear such tension is, of course, the "folly" of the cross. It is a selfless disposition in which you are no longer trying to prove that your side is right but are prepared to hang in the balance, between the good and bad thieves of every issue, for the sake of reconciliation. Only through this option can peace be achieved without forfeiting relationship.

Jesus stood in the gap between sin and God's law and bore, in His body, the reconciliation of both. "Go," our Lord says, "and do likewise."

> *For he himself is our peace, who has made the two one and has destroyed the barrier, the dividing wall of hostility, by abolishing in his flesh the law with its commandments and regulations. His purpose was to create in himself one new man out of the two, thus making peace, and in this one body to reconcile both of them to God through the cross, by which he put to death their hostility.*
>
> Eph. 2:14-16

65

43

*Love is patient, love is kind. It does not envy, it does not boast,
it is not proud. It is not rude, it is not self-seeking, it is not easily
angered, it keeps no record of wrongs. Love does not delight in
evil but rejoices with the truth......*

1 Cor. 13:4-6

The overall gist of Paul's famous list of attributes is clear—love is a pretty complex subject. Don't try and reduce it to just one thing, especially not to its more extreme expressions. When we think, for instance, of our love for God it's easy to picture ourselves worshipping the Lord with our hands raised (or not), our hearts pouring out affection, and our mouths singing praise. This is one overt expression of love, but it certainly isn't the most common one. Nor is it something that could be sustained for very long without soon becoming wearisome for both parties. Love is much more subtle than that.

Love nuances our many responses to life. It shades how we react to others, how we interpret and respond to them. It directs our movements. It holds us back at times, and moves us forward at other times.

Love is the desire to make whatever changes are needed in ourselves in order to remain close to someone. It's the corrective that we welcome in ourselves, for the sake of a more "fitting" relationship.

Love expresses itself not only as something offered, but mostly in how we receive the other person. It is the choice we make to let a person enter our lives, and stay there. It's what closes the doors to rejection.

Love gently tempers whatever excess it meets. It creates space and removes barriers by simply not entertaining anything that might deny it the right to receive the other person.

Love is the preferred option to bear discomfort for the sake of another. It is what we will willingly inconvenience ourselves for; what we will put up with; what we will ignore or overlook; and what we will take on at the expense of our own preferences.

Love is equilibrium. It is the ballast by which all other behaviours are adjusted. Though it often gets shaken out of its stability, love instills hope that life will always return to its original shape.

Love is all this, and many things more. It is important that we learn to recognize and celebrate its subtle forms as well as its more overt expressions.

> .....*it always protects, always trusts, always hopes, always perseveres. Love never fails.*
>
> 1 Cor. 13:7-8

44

> *Can a mother forget the baby at her breast and have no compassion on the child she has borne? Though she may forget, I will not forget you!*
>
> Isaiah 49:15

St. John of the Cross expressed a beautiful metaphor for our progressive awareness of God in the image of a mother's love for her baby. It is one that affirms both the constant nature of God's love, as well as the evolution of our response to that love as we mature in our faith.

When a baby is newborn it is not yet consciously aware of its mother's presence, other than that its basic needs are being met. For months following its birth, the mother often holds the baby in her arms and gazes lovingly at her child. Though the love that flows from the mother is directed towards it, the baby is not yet responsive to that love.

As the baby matures however, it gradually becomes aware of the mother's loving attention. As it anticipates her affection, the infant begins responding more and more to the experience of being dawdled upon. It giggles and responds to the mother's affection, loving the very idea of being loved.

But it is only later, when it is more mature, that the infant begins to respond lovingly to the mother's affection on its own initiative. It now recognizes both the mother's love that is directed towards it, as well as its own capacity to return that love. Throughout each of these stages of development, whether the child was responsive or not, the mother's love has remained constant. But it is only at this point that it can be said that the child is in a reciprocal, loving relationship with its mother

Every minute of every day God is similarly gazing upon us, loving us as a mother would her newborn baby. At some point in our maturity we too become aware of this love being directed towards us. We awaken to the reality that we are the object of love, and we delight in the experience and warmth of the Lord's affection for us. As we mature however, we grow beyond simply loving the *experience* of being loved, and we find more and more creative ways to reciprocate the affection that God has for us—we return love for love.

The apostle John says that, "we love God because He first loved us" (1Jn 4:19). Our spiritual maturity becomes established as we, in response to Divine love, grow in our capacity to "love the Lord our God with all our heart and with all our soul and with all our mind." Like the "weaned child" of David's affection, we bask in the recognition of love received, as well as in our mature desire and capacity to reciprocate it.

> *I have stilled and quieted my soul within me.*
> *Like a weaned child with its mother is my soul within me.*
>
> Psalm 131

45

> *Lands that drinks in the rain often falling on it, and that produces a crop useful for those for whom it was farmed, receives the blessing of God.*
>
> Heb. 6:7

According to this passage God's blessing seems to follow an ecological cycle. Like land that often gets showered with rain, we too are often blessed with optimum conditions and opportunities for growth. Each day we have occasion to drink this rain deeply into our lives. And, like any well-watered garden, we eventually produce a crop, the result of the Lord's blessings showered upon us.

But it doesn't stop there. According to this Scripture, the crop that we grow is not only for our own benefit. It is especially a blessing to "those for whom it was farmed." In other words, God grows a crop in us that is primarily designed for someone else's good.

Consider how this might apply to you. What has God cultivated in your life that is ultimately designed for someone else's sake? Is it a talent? A knack for hospitality or money-making? A cheerful disposition? A sober outlook?

It is both humbling as well as freeing to think that much of what you are—the crop of your life—has actually been given to you for the benefit of others. How does this change your relationship to God's blessings—to know that they belong more to others than to you? How might it motivate you differently in the cultivation of your gifts?

People will often do far greater things for the sake of others than they would ever do for themselves. They might acquire new skills, study a discipline, learn a craft or overcome certain fears or insecurities simply because others need them to do so. These are some of the ways that land, which "drinks in the rain often falling on it," bears fruit for the sake of others.

As we produce such an other-oriented crop in our lives we participate in the cycle of blessing which concludes, according to this passage, with the reward of yet more blessing from God. Presumably this blessing comes once again in the form of good rain showering upon us, which starts the cycle all over again. *Rain falls... we drink it in... a crop grows... others are blessed by it... more rain falls... we drink it in again... another crop grows.....*

46

There was given me a thorn in my flesh, a messenger of Satan, to torment me. Three times I pleaded with the Lord to take it away from me. But he said to me, "My grace is sufficient for you, for my power is made perfect in weakness." Therefore I will boast all the more gladly about my weaknesses, so that Christ's power may rest on me.

2 Cor. 12:7-9

How often do we presume that God's work is somehow limited by our deficiencies? For those who long for transformation, how prevalent in our thinking is the assumption that our progress will somehow translate into more opportunity for God? I suspect that this was a big part of Paul's motivation in pleading with God to remove the "thorn" he recognized in his flesh—that it was something that made him a less effective servant of the God he loved. It is easy to think in these terms isn't it? As though God's purposes were somehow impeded by the quality or quantity of what we have to offer.

If it was out of such concern that Paul so desperately prayed that this thorn be removed, we can certainly understand how he might've been disappointed, at first, by the response he got. The Lord never even acknowledged the issue that Paul identified. Instead, Jesus took occasion to express the sufficiency of His grace—as something that is not fostered, enabled, nor limited by Paul's disposition towards it.

For Paul, the Lord's answer to his prayer was yet another Damascus experience. In the space of two verses he expresses the full conversion of his weakness—from being the subject of his tormented plea, to now becoming the very object of his boast. Without it ever being removed from his life, Paul's "thorn" was nevertheless redeemed. It was transformed from an impediment, into something that actually increased glory for the Lord he loved.

Is God limited by the quality or quantity of what we have to offer? It seems not. Can even our weaknesses be Christ-glorifying? It would seem wonderfully so. Let us, like Paul, learn to delight in the paradox of such amazing grace.

47

Precious in the sight of the Lord is the death of his saints.
Psalm 116:15

Imagine the precious hour of your own death. What relationship do you think you will want to have with God at this moment? What type of familiarity, confidence or trust will you hope to have cultivated with the Lord by now?

No matter what age you are, it is good preparation to ask how you might apply your life today to that which will best serve you at your final hour. Consider this inevitable moment in your life and what relationship you might want to have developed with the Maker you will someday meet. Here are some familiarities you might hope to have cultivated.

In the final realization that you are approaching God's judgment, where "everything hidden will be revealed," it will be good for you to have developed an honest acceptance of the whole truth of who you are. It will be especially important for you to be certain of your theology of salvation—that Jesus accepts you as you are, and that His sacrifice on the cross is truly sufficient to forgive all your sins. If you think you might wish you had more time to prepare yourself before meeting God, it might be a sign that you have missed the very point of Christ's sacrifice for you.

Perhaps, as you approach this greatest unknown, you will be glad to have cultivated a life-long disposition of yielding to God's will in all things. In these final moments, when all your faculties for self-direction are useless to you, it will be good to have developed faith in God's direct hand on your life, and confidence that His sure guidance will continue to lead you in this moment, as it always has.

If you have lived a life of detachment it will naturally be easier for you to accept loss than if you have always found your bearings according to what you do, or to the things you own. It will be good for you to have lived according to Job's sober remembrance that "naked I came into the world, and naked I will depart" (Job 1:20).

If you have any trust issues with God you will be glad to have taken the healing of your relationship seriously, while you could still do so at your own pace. It will be better to have developed a healthy and genuine relationship with God beforehand than to be approaching this moment of uncertainty with unnecessary fears and misgivings about the character of God.

It will be good as well to have learned how to genuinely accept the truth of God's particular love for you. If you are confident that you are preciously loved, it will make it much easier for you to abandon yourself into the Lord's arms than if you are uncertain how God really feels about you.

And finally, if throughout your life, it has been your disposition to offer all that you are and all that you do for the Lord's purposes, it will be natural, once again, to offer the time and means of your death as a final way to serve God's purposes in life. If you have given yourself in this way, you will have good reason to anticipate that whatever happens in this final stage of the journey will be in accordance with this prayer.

Lord, I will trust You.
Help me to journey beyond the familiar
And into the unknown.
Give me the faith to leave old ways
And break fresh ground with You.

Christ of the mysteries, I trust You
To be stronger than each storm within me.
I will trust in the darkness and know
That my times, even now, are in Your hand.

Tune my spirit to the music of heaven,
And somehow, make my obedience count for You.

—St. Brendan (Irish contemplative)

48

I wait for the LORD, my soul waits,
and in his word I put my hope.
My soul waits for the Lord
more than watchmen wait for the morning,

Psalm 130:5-6

We will never know the Lord's initiative in our lives if don't learn how to stop taking the initiative ourselves. This is one of the most important things that the practice of contemplative prayer teaches us—to wait, in order to receive from the Lord.

Contemplative prayer is a time we set aside each day in order to stop, listen, and seek the Lord's direct action in our lives. It is a time when we loosen the grip we have on our preconceptions, our plans and our life strategies in order to allow God's creative initiative to be revealed to us. It is also one of the rare times we get to ask not only what we are to do, but also who we are, and who God wishes us to become.

In prayer we place ourselves as a living sacrifice on the altar and we wait, confident that the Lord will receive our offering and use it for His good purposes. The offering of contemplative prayer, however, is something that needs to be kept in place, sometimes for a much longer period than we had anticipated. It is too easy, after we've placed our life on the altar, to remove it from there once we've grown impatient or have lost faith that God is actually there to receive it. We feel alone. We find ourselves becoming restless, or tempted with despair. After a short period of waiting, we often give up on the hope of God's initiative and resort, once again, to our own agenda.

But the person who sets out to "wait on the Lord" must inevitably pass through this desert of uncertainty. They must resist the temptation to prematurely withdraw their offering if they hope to ever see the dawn of God's initiative emerging.

In the desert of silent prayer, the contemplative learns to wait in the stillness of faith. Like a watchman, he anticipates the morning of God's subtle initiative. And, it is in this very act of waiting that his offering is perfected. As Andrew Murray once wrote,

> Waiting honours God by giving Him time to have His way with us. It is the highest expression of our faith in His goodness and faithfulness. It brings the soul towards perfect rest in the assurance that God is truly carrying on His work.

We watch and wait in faith because we anticipate the initiative of God's movement. As the practice of such patience becomes easier for us, we will increasingly come to know the immediacy of God's faithfulness in our lives.

49

Take my yoke upon you and learn from me, for I am gentle and humble in heart, and you will find rest for your souls.

Matt. 11:29

Let us consider gentleness and its place in relationship to prayer and to the spiritual life. Gentleness is a quality that Jesus identifies with His own character and one which He invites us to share, as though yoked together, with Him.

The spirit of gentleness is what our prayer life ultimately produces in us. It comes from, as well as leads us to, a place of rest. Such was St. Frances de Sales' experience of gentleness in prayer.

> As I pray, I perceive deep within me a certain sweetness, tranquility, and a gentle repose of my spirit in divine Providence, which spreads abroad in my heart a great contentment, even in its pains.

Gentleness is a disposition that gives a beautiful grace to life. It is wonderfully free of the anxious grip of imperatives as it lets itself be led by the slightest breeze of the Spirit. As the 16th century spiritual director, Francis Fénelon taught, "A humble heart is always gentle and capable of being easily led in its center."

In its essence, gentleness represents the courage of faith. It is a bold statement to the principalities and powers above that we rest secure in the hand of God, since faith has freed us from our fears. Only the faith-filled man or woman can afford to risk such gentleness in life.

As we allow ourselves to be yoked with Jesus in this virtue, we will experience transformation in all of our relationships, including our relationship with ourselves. As Henri Nouwen puts it, "Through prayer we will learn the mastery of the gentle hand. Under this gentle regime, we will find ourselves once again becoming masters of our own house."

50

> Then a great and powerful wind tore the mountains apart and shattered the rocks before the LORD, but the LORD was not in the wind. After the wind there was an earthquake, but the LORD was not in the earthquake. After the earthquake came a fire, but the LORD was not in the fire. And after the fire came a gentle whisper.
>
> 1 Kings 19:11-12

Most of us tend to look for God's guidance in the big sweeps of life. What job should I take? Which church should I attend? Who should I marry? There is, of course, divine guidance for us in these important matters. But like Elijah who, at first, sought the Lord's word through the larger expressions of life—in the metaphors of strong winds and earthquakes—we often find that the more subtle, day to day work of the Holy Spirit actually takes place in the metaphor of gentle, but constant, whispers.

To sense the daily nudges of the Holy Spirit guiding you on your path is something that can be easily gained through the cultivation of prayerful attentiveness. An ongoing practice of prayer helps you recognize the movements of spirit that are, and have always been, taking place in the foundations of your life. Though it may only be a fleeting experience, there is nothing more reassuring than to be reminded that, moment by moment, whether you are aware of it or not, God is guiding you.

As Elijah discovered, it is the practice of stillness that makes us more attentive to the subtle whispers of God. Awareness of this gentle movement brings with it not only guidance but also the confidence that, even when we don't perceive it, this action is still taking place within us.

As we grow in relationship to God's active presence within us we will come to appreciate more and more the ministry of our Creator, whose hand is always on the rudder of our hearts. With simple adjustments here and there He is constantly directing the navigations of our lives.

51

In building the temple, only blocks dressed at the quarry were used, and no hammer, chisel or any other iron tool was heard at the temple site while it was being built.

1 Kings 6:7

Solomon built a Temple for God. In hindsight, the writers of the New Testament understood it as a symbol of the heavenly Temple that, as living stones, we are being fashioned into. This particular verse from 1Kings reveals an important feature in the construction of the Temple that might shed light on the relationship between life on earth and our future role as "bricks" in God's edifice.

The sanctuary that Solomon built was mostly made of large pre-fab stones. Each stone had been hewn and squared at the quarry, and its particular place in the building predetermined long before it was shipped to Jerusalem. In his building strategy it would seem that Solomon followed his own advice in Prov. 24:27: "Prepare thy work without, and make it fit for thyself in the field; and afterwards build thine house." (KJV).

With foresight as to where each should go, every stone was carefully pre-shaped according to the precise directions of the master architect. Once the stones were brought in, they were so perfectly fit for their place that neither hammer nor axe was heard in the Temple while it was being built. Everything came together in relative peace and quiet. Nothing needed to be altered or amended as all the rough work had already been done in the field prior to assembly.

It would seem that, on this side of heaven, we too are being made fit in the field. There is a precise work being carried out by the Master Builder upon His living stones. We too are being dressed according to the specific needs of the Architect-being, as it were, pre-fit for heaven. In this life we certainly experience many forms of "hammers, chisels or iron tools" that God uses to fashion us according to our designated place. And it is often pretty noisy business. On the other side however, where God's Temple will finally be assembled, no such clamour will be necessary. No more will preaching, exhortations, repentance, vows, prophecies or corrections be uttered or heard. No coercion will be needed. No alterations required.

Each stone will have already been perfectly squared and fitted for its particular place in the New Jerusalem.

It is in quietness and peace that the habitation of God, who always works in tranquility, will finally be established. It is no wonder then that stillness and rest are such an integral part of prayer. They prepare us for the ambience of silence in which we will each find our proper place in God's holy city.

> . . . *You also, like living stones, are being built into a spiritual house to be a holy priesthood . . .*
>
> 1 Pet. 2:5

52

Whoever finds his life will lose it, and whoever loses his life for my sake will find it.

Matt. 10:39

Of all the saints who have ever walked in the imitation of Christ, the life of St. Francis of Assisi certainly represents a wonderful model of the potential we have for making radical changes in our lives. His biography offers us an inspiring example of what is possible in a life that responds fully to the call to conversion.

After hearing the Gospel invitation, Francis, the son of a rich man, immediately gave all his possessions away to the poor. When his father brought him before the Bishop in order to have him chastised for this wasteful behaviour Francis responded by immediately removing the few remaining clothes he had on him, giving them back to his father, and then walking out of the church naked.

After once again accumulating some of the bare necessities of life, Francis later heard a sermon about Jesus' call to His disciples to "take no bag for the journey, or extra tunic, or sandals or staff.' Francis' immediate response was to leave his staff and sandals behind at the church and devote himself from this point on to a life of extreme poverty.

On another occasion later in his life, Francis came to recognize the natural repulsion he felt whenever he was confronted by a leper in the streets. Like most people of his day, he avoided contact with them at all costs. Confronted by Jesus in this matter, Francis immediately changed his attitude, and now even went out of his way to be among the lepers, hugging and kissing them as evidence of his transformation.

As with Francis, God has also confronted each one of us about changes He is calling forth in our lives. What energy do we find for conversion in these? How whole-hearted is our response? How subtle are we at finding ways to ignore or put off these invitations rather than taking the radical steps necessary for change?

For Francis, the recognition of a God-identified need for conversion was the immediate cause for a drastic lifestyle change. He did not pray about the issue, waiting for God to motivate him. He did not try to chip away at his fault, hoping to eventually see progress. Instead, Francis immediately re-oriented his life away from his fault, and towards the most opposite direction he could imagine. In so doing he was able to turn each of his weaknesses into a source for his greatest strengths. Anyone who has ever been touched by this humble saint recognizes Francis as a God-sent model of what true conversion in a life can really look like.

53

The LORD is God, and he has made his light shine upon us.
With boughs in hand, join in the festal procession
up to the horns of the altar.

Psalm 118:26-27

All along the 1500km of the Camino de Santiago pilgrimage route in France and Spain there are convents, monasteries and churches that provide hospitality to those who seek food and lodging at the end of a day. Priests, monks, nuns and lay volunteers minister to the needs of weary travelers, providing food, shelter and spiritual direction to all who seek it. For pilgrims who walk this historic route, the experience of being cared for by these dedicated people is one of the highlights of their journey. And there are many who would love to linger longer at one of these sites if they could.

As a spiritual director, I was most intrigued by this extremely fluid form of church ministry. Like a river flowing through its doors, new "congregants" show up every day at these hostels. The people are ministered to and then sent off to continue their pilgrimage, now rested and refreshed. As much as a person might like to linger, the church insists that you stay no more than two nights, and then you must resume your pilgrimage. There is something about this model of ministry that resonates deeply with my instincts for church—as a place that perhaps ministers best to its people by kicking them out of the building and sending them back to continue their spiritual journey.

This is, of course, a very different concept of the church than we are used to. It is much more tempting for us to try to make a home, or a city out of the church. And it is also just as tempting for the church to try to accumulate assets, namely people, as a sign of its viability. But what if, as

Psalm 118 reminds us, the main purpose of our pilgrimage is to "join in the festal procession" all the way up to the horns of the altar? If this is the case then it is important that we encourage one another to keep returning to the road, and not let ourselves be lulled into setting up camp before we reach the altar's horns.

There are, of course, many reasons why a ministry with an ever-changing congregation could never really constitute a church body. But the role of sending people back out on the road, as one of the ways we minister to them, is perhaps a helpful corrective for any church, or believer, who has forgotten that Christianity is meant to be "the Way"—a path more than a place of refuge.

54

Dear friend, I pray that you may enjoy good health and that all
may go well with you, even as your soul is getting along well.

3 John1:2

What a beautiful thing to wish for ourselves or for one another—that "your soul is getting along well." What do we think John meant by this phrase, and what are some of the alternatives to a soul "getting along well" that might be possible in life?

A quick look through a Scripture concordance can tell us a lot about the soul—how it operates and what its capacities are. And getting a better sense of how the Biblical writers have used this word can give us a very interesting composite of what the Bible means by "soul." It also makes it clear why we should not take it for granted that our souls are "getting along well."

Many things can, and often do, detract a soul from an otherwise healthy state. We learn from the Scriptures that the soul suffers (Isa. 53:11) and can be distressed (Ps. 77:2). It can be forlorn (Ps. 35:12), downcast (Ps 42:5-6), troubled (Ps. 88:3) or grieved (Job 30:25). It experiences anguish (Psalm 6:3, 31:7) and can grow weary with sorrow (Ps. 119:28). The soul can become bitter (Job 3:20, 7:11, Sam. 1:16) and even has the capacity to hate (Ps. 11:5). These are some of the very real experiences of the soul that we share with the Biblical writers. We can see why John doesn't take for granted the fact that his friend's soul is getting along well.

Though the soul can at times be weak (Psalm 31:9); though it hungers, thirsts (Ps. 42:1-2, 63:1), yearns and even faints (Ps. 84:2, 119:81), by the grace of God, it can also be re-awakened (Ps. 57:8), revived and restored (Ps. 19:7, 23:3). In all this we get a sense that the soul can be subject to both good and poor health at times. We are encouraged to take seriously the need to care for and protect our souls (Pr. 22:5) so that they can be free to do what they are ultimately designed for—to love and to rejoice in God always (Ps. 35:9, Isa. 61:10).

To ask yourself, and each other, how your soul is getting along is indeed a very practical question. Spiritual wisdom will help us maintain good spiritual health as we learn how to protect the soul from unnecessary turmoil and dis-ease. And a healthy state of soul will preserve for us the wonderful foretaste of God in our present life.

55

Six days you shall labor, but on the seventh day you shall rest;
even during the plowing season and harvest you must rest.

Ex. 34:21

Leaves changing colours in the fall are always a feast to the eyes. They delight our senses and imaginations, and have provided poets, preachers and prophets with countless metaphors of life and death. My wife Ruth, who works for a Christian conservation organization (www. arocha.org) taught me something important about how the changing colours in a leaf are also related to the beauty we discover in ourselves whenever we rest in God.

During the summer months, when the sun is closer to the earth, leaves are busy providing the tree with glucose. The sunlight helps the leaves transform water and carbon dioxide into a kind of sugar that the tree needs in order to live and grow. This process of photosynthesis (which literally means "putting together with light") activates a chemical in the leaf called chlorophyll, which is what gives the leaf its green colour. This, of course, is rudimentary knowledge for most. But perhaps the association of the green in a leaf, as the colour of work, might be new for you.

As summer ends and the days get shorter, there is not enough light nor water for photosynthesis to continue. The trees rest from their work and now live off the energy that has been stored over the summer. As the "work engines" shut down, the green chlorophyll disappears from the leaves and now the yellow, orange and red are revealed—colours that have always been present in the leaf, but were covered over by the green hue of summer activity. The leaves now display their beautiful autumn palette—their colours of rest.

Consider how this phenomenon relates to the changing seasons of your own life—the daily, weekly, monthly or yearly patterns of work and rest that you enjoy. The "green" seasons in our lives—our work colours—are, of course, also beautiful to behold. They represent the vitality of all the productive work going on in and around us. But, every autumn, the Lord reminds us, through the changing leaves, that there are other beautiful colours inside us as well, lying just beneath the surface of our work colours. In order for those colours to be revealed we need only stop our work and allow time for the yellows, oranges and reds colours of rest to come to the fore. It's a pretty easy recipe for uncovering beauty in yourself.

Throughout the year, may we all enjoy days and seasons of Sabbath when we too can display the wonderful array of our restful colours. It will bring as much delight to those around us as the autumn foliage brings us each fall.

56

But blessed are your eyes because they see, and your ears because they hear.

Matt. 13:16

Years ago, when I studied portrait painting, I was always mystified when the teacher would speak of the shades of purple and green that she could so easily detect in the shadows around the face and head. To my untrained eyes, shadows along the neck or in the eye socket simply looked gray. There are, of course, many subtle hues of light within a shadow, but it took years of cultivating a sensitivity to this light before I could ever appreciate the beauty my teacher recognized.

Similarly, there are many subtleties of divine presence and movement all around us that often escape our notice. As the Jesuit author, William Barry notes,

> Whether we are aware of it or not, at every moment of our existence we are encountering God, who is trying to catch our attention, trying to draw us into a reciprocal conscious relationship.

The soul is the God-given "sense" through which we recognize the divine actions that grace every moment of our existence. Like the eye that detects the presence of light, and the nose that recognizes fragrance, the soul similarly identifies the presence of God within and around us. And, as men and women throughout Christian history have discovered, our souls have a capacity to grow in their sensitivity to divine activity.

The metaphors that are often used to describe the qualities and capacities of the soul would indicate that it operates, in many ways, like our natural senses do. When the Bible tells us, for instance, to "taste and see that the Lord is good" (Ps. 34:8) it is not referring to our literal taste buds, nor to our eyesight, but to a particular sense of the soul that is related, metaphorically, to our natural senses of taste and sight. Similarly, when the Scripture speaks of "listening" to the Lord it is referring to a particular form of hearing that, though similar to the one we know of through our ears, is such that only our souls are capable of.

Our natural senses gather information much like a satellite dish receives radio signals. They magnify for us the smells, sights, sounds, flavours and tactile presences in this world by focusing our attention on them. In the same way, our souls seem to be able to "detect" the presence of the Lord. They "hear," "see," "taste," "smell," and "touch" information from God which then allows us to discern what is being communicated.

A satellite dish needs to be set up and carefully adjusted in order to pick up the particular signals you wish it to receive. Perhaps our souls also need to be properly "aimed" in order to best receive the information they seek. That is why the Scriptures so often urge us to seek and desire God above all things—so that our souls will be focused to recognize the beauty of the Lord that is otherwise hidden in the shadows of life.

So how are we to more fully enjoy the blessings that Jesus refers to—of having ears that truly hear and eyes that see such beauty in and around us? Perhaps it is as simple a matter as William Barry suggests when he says that, "the religious dimension of experience is encountered mostly by the person of faith who is on the alert for God." Intentionality, it would seem, is the mother of reception.

Jesus claims that we are already blessed with souls that have the capacity to see, hear, taste, smell and touch God. Let us grow then in this sense-itive, living experience of our Father, who delights in catching the attention of His children.

57

The mountains melt like wax before the LORD, before the Lord of all the earth.

Psalm 97:5

If mountains melt like wax before the Lord, it is no wonder that our hearts do as well. Many of our most profound experiences of God are also often accompanied by physiological responses—sensations of peace, warmth and well-being.* And it is often through these responses that we discover, once again, how very tender and fluid our hearts can be as they "melt like wax" before the Lord.

While a candle is burning, the hardened wax turns to liquid and either makes a pool under the flame, or else begins to flow freely down the candlestick. Once the flame is extinguished however, or the wax has dripped below the range of its heat, it hardens into whatever form it has cooled down to. We know that it will remain in this state until the candle is lit again, and the heat of the flame causes the wax to melt and be fluid once more.

Our hearts, as well, "harden" into various shapes whenever they are away from the light of God for too long. We feel stuck, unfree, not as fluid as we once were. As we return to God however, we sense something loosening up within us. This is often our experience when we worship,

---

* This is not to say that our experience of God is the only indicator of His presence, nor that the lack of an experience of God implies His absence. It is simply to recognize the fact that spiritual experience, when it does occur, is often accompanied by physiological signs.

read Scripture, or pray in the presence of God. Our hearts warm up to the Lord's light and begin to "melt" before Him.

There is another image of wax that also helps identify this dynamic of spiritual life. For those who have never heard of a lava lamp, this curiosity was an enclosed, glass lamp with a light bulb at its base. The glass was filled with oil, with a large blob of wax floating in it. As the wax sank to the bottom of the glass it was heated up by the light bulb and would then slowly start floating upwards. All sorts of mesmerizing shapes were created as the wax broke apart and reformed in wonderfully indeterminate ways. Once it got to the top, away from the direct heat of the light bulb, it would cool down and start descending again through the oil. The wax would dance up and down the lamp like this, depending on how close it was to the heat of the lamp.

The most curious aspect of a lava lamp is how such a mindless activity could, for inordinately long periods of time, delight those watching it. What was it that made such a phenomenon so attractive? Perhaps, in the ebb and flow of the wax to the heat of the light, we subconsciously recognized something familiar—a similar movement in our own souls as they move towards and away from God.

Like wax being warmed by a flame, or else cooling down when it is distant, our hearts are always changing according to their relationship to God's light. It is because our Father wants us to enjoy a freely-flowing life that we are repeatedly invited to draw near the warmth of His presence, where we are told that even hardened things like mountains end up melting like wax.

58

The mind controlled by the Spirit is life and peace.

Rom. 8:6

Prayer often begins in the mind. The decision to pray is usually followed by thoughts of what to do about it, a reflection perhaps of the purpose of what we are doing, and a recall of methods and means that we believe will help us in that purpose. But the mind itself cannot lead us to contemplative prayer. By its very nature it hovers above the spirit—observing, learning, and informing the will. It can never become, nor lead us to our souls.

But often, as our prayer progresses, we recognize the presence of another Guide. From the place of stillness, the subtleties of the Holy Spirit are revealed in the heart. In a gentle, interior movement that is usually imperceptible to the mind, the Spirit of love, peace and spiritual joy now offers to lead us In the direction of deeper prayer. We are invited to follow its ways, and therein begins the gradual transformation of our desires—from the desire to know, to the desire to "be." The mind, now controlled by the spirit, promises to lead us to an experience of life and peace that we could never attain on our own.

Contemplative prayer that emerges from the heart is of a quality that is immediately recognized as more profound in truth and essence than any other form of knowledge. Though foreign at first, its language is one that resonates with the deepest instincts of our being. We sense as well that it represents an opportunity to re-identify ourselves according to this new, and truer center from which we can learn afresh who we are, and where we are going.

Once we have recognized the deeper self within us it is very difficult to return to anything less. We now have an experience of profound life as revealed to us by the Spirit, and we become more acutely aware whenever we stray from this place of deeper truth. A subtle tension results when we become aware that we are no longer operating from our center, and this tension beckons us to keep returning to the deeper truth that we know exists within us. It is this tension, and our continual response to it, that gradually re-habituates us towards a deeper place of origin—a place born of the Spirit, rather than of ourselves.

Once this pearl has been identified as precious, we more naturally and willingly respond to God's invitation to exchange all we have for all He wishes to give us. We choose, even if it means letting go of our familiar habits of thought, to let our minds be more and more controlled by the Spirit.

*The mind controlled by the spirit...*Imagine the different experience of life that this new order will offer us. In submission to the Holy Spirit, we are told that we will find rest and renewal in the freedom that God has saved us for.

59

But you, brothers and sisters, are not in darkness so that this day should surprise you like a thief.

1 Thes. 5:4

In his letter to the Thessalonians, Paul writes about the return of the Lord. In response to many questions the church had on this issue he describes, in more detail than anywhere else, the events that will surround this Advent hope. It is perhaps difficult for us to relate to this being as pressing an issue as it was for the Thessalonians, and yet the imminent return of the Lord is clearly one of the most oft-repeated teachings of Jesus,. Throughout the New Testament two certainties of eschatology are often emphasized—that the Lord will return one day, and that it will catch us all by surprise.

Paul tells us to stay alert lest this occasion should surprise us like a thief coming in the night. But what exactly would this "thief" steal from us? It doesn't take much stretch of an imagination to realize that, if Jesus were to return today, it would be our dreams, our plans and all the expectations we have for this life that would appear to be suddenly stolen from us. All our best-laid plans would immediately become irrelevant and, if we were not in the right spiritual disposition, the Lord's coming could represent for us a day of great loss rather than the joy of a new beginning that it truly is.

How will even the Lord's own people receive His coming? It is quite possible that His return might bring joy to some and disappointment to others. Just imagine some likely responses. "Jesus has returned? Oh no. I just got married....I'm in the middle of a church plant.... I've been saving up for my European holiday and we're just getting ready to go.... I'm in the middle of some important negotiations and we just need a bit more time.....I'm been working on my self-esteem issues for years and I'm just starting to see some progress....I've almost reached my goals....I just need more time!"

It's easy to live in the illusion that the loose threads of our personal stories, or those on the world's stage, must all be somehow resolved before life, as we know it, comes to an end. But Scripture clearly states that the Lord will come not at the end of these stories, but in the very midst of them. People will be in the middle of the busy-ness of marriage preparations, of buying and selling, of making plans for tomorrow. And, in an instant, all these stories will come to an abrupt end. Are we prepared to have this happen? Are we ready to drop all the details of our lives in order to run out and meet our Lord? Or will it seem as if a thief has robbed us of all our earthly hopes and ambitions?

Paul says that we should know better than to let this day surprise us as a thief.

> You are all children of the light and children of the day. We do not belong to the night or to the darkness. So then, let us not be like others, who are asleep, but let us be alert and self-controlled. (1 Thes. 5:5-6)

We have occasion, each Advent, to meditate on the Lord's coming. If we can honestly say that we are prepared, at any moment, to exchange our story for His—to receive the Lord, not as a thief, but as the Author of the joyful new beginning that is about to unfold at His return—it is a sure sign that we have not fallen asleep to this most important truth.

60

What a man desires is unfailing love; better to be poor than a liar
Prov. 19:22

People who pray regularly recognize and must accept that they don't always desire God as much as they wish they did. It is an uncomfortable truth that requires a certain amount of courage before we can even admit it to ourselves. But once we do—once we accept that we are weak in our desires for God—a new path opens up for us. We come to recognize that it is "better to be poor than a liar."

From such a place of honesty we are now free to choose whether a genuine desire for God is something that we really wish to have or not. If it isn't, then at least we are being true with ourselves and can now ask God to continue working in us so that this might someday become something we actually desire. Perhaps this is the very "poverty of spirit" that Jesus spoke of as, paradoxically, a blessed state. If, however, a desire for God is something that we do wish for ourselves, then we simply and earnestly have to begin asking for it.

If, in examining ourselves, we recognize that our hearts have become tepid, it is quite legitimate for us to take a step back and pray for the desire to desire. If we feel that we have lost our passion, we can simply be honest about it and ask the Holy Spirit to increase our desire for God, to restore us to our first love, or to wean us away from the things that now distract us.

A sincere desire for God is something that can always be restored to us. But, before that can happen, it might be necessary for us to first recognize and admit to ourselves that it is absent.

> *O Jesus, my desires are often weak and wayward, and I don't know what I can do about it. I wish to see them increase and to have my life directed more towards what I know I desire most—You.*
>
> *Thank You Lord that this relationship does not wholly depend on me. For I know that I would be lost and without hope if it did.*
>
> *Thank You that You continually create for me the path that I am to follow. There is nowhere else from which to begin this path than from where I am right now.*
>
> *Thank You that, though You call me to seek You, You also reveal Yourself as the One who has already found me. In such faith, I know I am saved. Amen.*

61

In righteousness you will be established.

Isaiah 54:14

To be "righteous" implies being in right relationship to all things. It is what establishes us in life, literally "making us stable." Through the sanctifying ministry of the Holy Spirit, Jesus encourages us towards relational righteousness in all areas of our life. He is continually making adjustments in areas where we are either over-related or under-related to the life around us.

You don't have to be a close friend with everyone you meet, nor do you have to be passionate about every good cause, but you do have to seek God in order to ensure that you are in right relationship to all He has placed around you.

As an inspiration for prayer, the Jesuit model of the Awareness Examen is something that can easily be applied to our relationships. It is a simple exercise of scanning the particulars of your life and asking the Holy Spirit to reveal to you areas of consolation and desolation in the ways you experience the diverse relationships that connect you to the world. Here's what such an Awareness Examen might look like:

An Examen of Relationships

As you seek to be rightly related to all things, take time to consider all the relationships in your life that this presently applies to. In this examen we ask God to first show us His pleasure in terms of the consolations we feel about certain relationships in our lives. Some of the facets we examine can include our relationship:

> to God,... to the church,... to those who love you,... to those who don't,... to yourself,... to your gifts,... to your shortcomings,... to your appetites,... to your sexuality,...to your spirituality,...to your work,...to rest,... to money,... to security,... to the future,... to your past,... to your desires,... to your fears,... to your dreams,... to your responsibilities,...to your life story so far,... to this present moment,... and so on.

You could add to this list anything else the Holy Spirit brings to mind regarding the consolations you experience in your present relationships.

In these same areas of your life, consider the relationships where you experience desolation. Ask the Holy Spirit to reveal to you places of disconnection in these same relationships:

> to God,... to the church,... to those who love you,... to those who don't,... to yourself,... and so on.

You could as well add to this list any other areas the Holy Spirit brings to mind regarding the desolations you experience in your present relationships.

Now ask Jesus, in whom all things are held together, to show you what righteousness means as applied to all the relationships of your life. Invite Him to adjust, wherever necessary, any places of disconnection, i.e. any inordinate relationship that He has revealed to you.

And finally, be prepared to participate with the correctives and promptings of the Holy Spirit in seeking, finding and living in right relationship to all areas of your life. The apostle Paul tells that, as much as is possible, we should seek to be at peace with all things (Rom. 12:18).

If we continually bring our relationships to Jesus for correction, He promises that He will lead us to righteousness in all matters. In Him, all things will come to fit together as they should.

62

The light shines in the darkness, but the darkness has not understood it.

John 1:5

Christmas offers Canadians a very literal expression of this Scripture. The days get colder, shorter and darker and then, all of a sudden, in the midst of the declining light, we get to celebrate once again the true Light of the world. The contrast itself makes the metaphor that this holiday represents all the more poignant. But what effect does this light, shining in our darkest season, have on those around us? How does God minister to the world, whether they know it or not, through this celebration of Jesus' birth?

Grace seems to abound at Christmas, so much so that you don't even have to believe in Christ in order to be blessed by it. It's as if all the stores, TV stations, newspapers and work places have been unwittingly conscripted into participating in this celebration of salvation history that has been dropped onto their lap. They're swept up in the party even if they don't know why.

Isaiah also celebrated our day when he envisioned that "the people walking in darkness have seen a great light; on those living in the land of the shadow of death a light has dawned" (Isa. 9:2). There are many around us who have not yet recognized this great Light shining on them. But for those on whom it has dawned, it is a wonder-filled gift. The light of Christ expands within us and will continue to do so "like the first gleam of dawn, shining ever brighter till the full light of day" (Prov. 4:18). This is the good news we anticipate for those around us as well.

Let us celebrate Jesus' birth among ourselves. But let us also delight in the effect Christmas has on an unsuspecting world. Whether it realizes the "reason for the season" or not, the world is still blessed by this celebration. Such is the lavish grace of God. Though the darkness has not yet understood it, the promise still stands that those who walk in the shadow of this Light will sense something of its presence dawning within their souls.

63

Listen and hear my voice; pay attention and hear what I say.
When a farmer plows for planting, does he plow continually?
Does he keep on breaking up and harrowing the soil? When
he has leveled the surface, does he not sow caraway and scatter
cumin? Does he not plant wheat in its place, barley in its plot,
and spelt in its field? His God instructs him and teaches him
the right way.

Isaiah 28:23-26

As Isaiah teaches, there are different stages to spiritual growth and each one is a necessary part of the whole cycle. You don't water a plant every day. Instead you must wait for its cycle of desire to come around again. When you see that it is dry—that it is showing signs of need—then you know it is time to water it once more.

Through nature, God teaches us the very same principles that He applies to our lives. In order to encourage growth, He creates both seasons of need and seasons of satisfaction within us. As you recall your experience of the past year consider the following:

What particular seasons of growth do you remember?

What were the dry times?

What circumstances occasioned these experiences?

What has grown in you as a result of these dry or abundant times?

What has been pruned as a result of these?

What new or deeper desires do you now have that you didn't a year ago?

What desires did you have then that don't seem to be as pressing today?

What do you now know about God that you didn't a year ago?

How is your relationship to others different than at this time last year?

As we grow in faith and attentiveness to the Lord's direct hand in our lives, let us consider how we can more fully welcome His creativity in the year ahead. How we can keep ourselves open, each hour of the day, to be molded and fashioned according to the Lord's particular will in us?

This, in essence, is the contemplative life and disposition—to be always trusting and submissive to God with regards to who you are, and to who, in His good purposes, you are becoming.

64

How beautiful on the mountains
*   are the feet of those who bring good news,*
*   who proclaim peace, who bring good tidings,*
*   who proclaim salvation, who say to Zion,*
*   "Your God reigns!"*

Isaiah 52:7

Many of us at Imago Dei are grateful to God for what we recognize as a very special experience of faith that we share together. And the more we appreciate the blessings of community the more natural the thought of how we might include others should be. To keep such things to ourselves would not only be selfish, it would be counter to the very movement of the Holy Spirit that we are enjoying. Who are the particular people in our midst for whom such an experience of faith might also be an encouragement? And how does one go about conveying God's invitation to them?

By virtue of being recipients of the Lord's grace we inevitably become ambassadors of that same grace. Moved by our love for friends and family we extend the Lord's invitation to "draw near to me" to all who will listen. Along with that invitation we also instill hope that, as they do, the Lord Himself will draw near to them. Not only do we extend this invitation but, by God's grace, we also embody the living proof—in our joy, confidence and enthusiasm—that such promises are true.

The feet of those who carry good news are truly beautiful because they are the feet of love and generosity. We cannot help but wish on others all that the Holy Spirit has blessed us with. We desire that they too would recognize and respond to God's ways within them. So we encourage those we love to respond to that call, to make time to seek God for themselves, and to explore the Spirit of the Lord that beckons them from within.

As we encourage our friends God-ward, we also listen with familiar understanding to their fears—to the trust issues they are working out with God. We empathize with them as we recognize, in their hesitations, the same fears that challenge our faith as well. But we also offer assurances from our experience that God is always near, that He is faithful, and that He loves us much more than we could ever imagine.

And so, with beautiful feet, we walk in the direction and formation of spiritual friendships with those we love. We present ourselves as fellow pilgrims, seekers committed to the journey who will joyfully share with them whatever spiritual food we find along the way. To be such a spiritual friend is the highest form of love we can offer or receive. Let us be so privileged as to become such a friend to those we love.

ABOUT IMAGO DEI

This is to my Father's glory, that you bear much fruit, showing yourselves to be my disciples.

John 15:8

Jesus bore fruit in individuals, making them His disciples, and then sent them out as ministers in the world—in the marketplace, in their families, among their fellow tradesmen, in their social circles and in their politics. The Lord promised to meet them in a special way whenever they gathered together, but it is clear that His expectations were that the ministry of His Presence and Word would take place as much in the world as among themselves.

As new Imago Dei groups take root in various places we often have to remind ourselves what the fruit of our small ministry is. In a nutshell, the ministry of Imago Dei is not about itself—it's about you, and the fruit you bear as a result of your intimate relationship with Jesus. The ministry of Imago Dei is a means to an end, and not an end in itself. By encouraging your life with Christ, and by creating resources to help you grow in this calling, the hope is that your own God-encouraged ministry will flourish as a result.

It's easy to think of vocation as the prime expression of our lives, as though once we have identified this we need only pour ourselves into it. But spirituality is the real fuel of ministry. Seeking God each day as the wellspring of our lives is the necessary fount for the work we are called to do in this world.

The contemplative pursuit encourages us to find and remain in that place of honest communication with God—the place where our spiritual identities are created, restored and constantly adjusted. The spirit of prayer is the ground from which our active life must be defined and re-defined if it is truly to originate from God. Ultimately our ministry is not what we do, but who we are in the various places God has assigned us.

Community, of course, is essential to our being rooted in the life of the Spirit and we encourage you, wherever you are, to band together with others who share your sincere desire for a more immediate walk with God. Such people are a rare gift to your life—there to remember God's Presence to you. As you allow them to do so, the company of those who know and affirm you will help you be more constant in your spiritual life.

If we can be of any help in encouraging such small communities in your locale please feel free to contact us through our website, www. imagodeicommunity.ca.

Rob Des Cotes
Imago Dei Christian Community

BIBLIOGRAPHY
OF WORKS CITED

Eugene Peterson, *Christ Plays in Ten Thousand Places,* (Grand Rapids, Mich.: Wm. Eerdmans Publishing., 2005)

St. John of the Cross, *The Dark Night of the Soul* (London: Hodder & Stoughton, 1988).

William Barry, S.J,. *Finding God in All Places* (Notre Dame, Ill.: Ave Maria Press, 1991)

Thaddée Matura, O.F.M., *Francis of Assisi* (Cincinnati, Ohio: St. Anthony Messenger Press, 2005)

Rohr, Richard, *Hope Against Darkness: the Transforming Vision of St. Francis in an Age of Anxiety,* (Cincinnati, Ohio: St. Anthony Messenger Press, 2001)

Carlo Carretto, *In Search of the Beyond,* (London: Darton, Longman and Todd Ltd., 1975)

James Houston, *Joyful Exiles* (Downers Grove, Ill.: Intervarsity Press, 2006)

Evelyn Underhill, *Mysticism* (Mineola, NY: Dover Publications, 2002)

Fr. Thomas Keating, *Open Heart, Open Mind* (NY, Continuum Press, 1986)

Matthew the Poor, *Orthodox Prayer Life* (Crestwood, NY: St. Vladimir's Seminary Press, 2003).

The Philokalia, translated by G.E.H. Palmer, Philip Sherrard and Kallistos Ware, (London: Faber and Faber, 1995)

Sayings of the Desert Fathers, translated by Benedicta Ward, SLG (Kalamazoo, Mich.: Cistercian Publications 1975)

Janet Ruffing, *Spiritual Direction; Beyond the Beginnings* (Mahwah, NJ: Paulist Press, 2000)

Ignatius of Loyola, *The Spiritual Exercises of St. Ignatius,* translated by Louse J. Puhl, S.J. (Chicago, Ill.: Loyola Press, 1951)

François Fénélon, *Talking with God* (Brewster, Mass.: Paraclete Press, 1997).

Anonymous, The Theologia Germanica of Martin Luther, translated by Susanna Winkworth, (Mineola, NY: Dover Publications, 2004)

Thomas Merton, *Thoughts in Solitude* (Boston, Mass.: Shambala Press, 1993)

St. Francis de Sales, *Thy Will Be Done* (Manchester, N.H.: Sophia Press, 1995).

Thomas Green, S.J. *Weeds Among the Wheat* (Notre Dame, Ill.: Ave Maria Press, 1984)

SCRIPTURE INDEX

Printed in the United States
94985LV00003B/259-336/A